D0916732

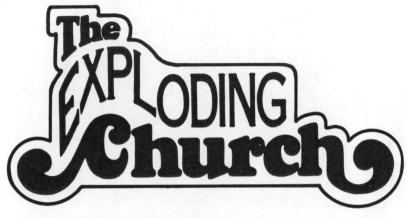

by

Thomas F. Reid

with

Doug Brendel

Logos International
Plainfield, New Jersey

The Exploding Church
Copyright ©1979 Logos International
All rights reserved
Printed in the United States of America
Library of Congress Catalog Card Number: 78-73575
International Standard Book Number: 0-88270-299-8
Logos International, Plainfield, New Jersey 07060

DEDICATION

To my staff, deacons, church leaders and congregation who have shown their love for the past fifteen years. It is their dedication that has made our ministry a success;

and

To my wife, Wanda, who has so fully shared her life with mine.

Contents

Preface

On repeated occasions during the past few years it has been my pleasure to share ministry with Pastor Tommy Reid and the saints unto whom God has given this man as a pastor.

If ever a congregation has experienced the fulfillment of Habakkuk's prayer, this group of believers has. "O Lord," he prayed, "revive Your work in the midst of the years, in the midst of the years make Yourself known!" (Hab. 3:2 TAB). That the Full Gospel Tabernacle is a revived, turned-on church is evident even to the casual observer. Its worship is vibrant with life, and the interpersonal relationships among the people are characterized by love.

But to those of us who have had the opportunity to see behind the scenes, the greater work of God is to be observed in the lives of the pastoring staff. They are dedicated to the work of the Lord and to each other. They seem to share a common vision and a similar anointing. Pastor Reid shares both the glory and the gold with his staff, for he is convinced that the staff is there in the will of the Lord as surely as he is, and that they should function "as one man."

The Exploding Church is must reading for every pastor and genuinely concerned layman, for this story is repeatable.

Judson Cornwall
Author and Bible Teacher

Introduction

I first met Tommy Reid in 1962. Young and handsome, he traveled to various countries around the world in preaching campaigns. Even then, Tommy Reid was a man marked with a message; his meetings in Korea were fruitful and blessed with the moving of the Holy Spirit.

Since that time he has gone through many changes and shifts in concepts and practices that have revolutionized his life and ministry. This is a book about those changes, written by a true servant of the Lord, with obvious sensitivity to the Spirit. It is because of this sensitivity that God has been able to mold him into a tremendous vessel, using him to develop an outstanding work in the city of Buffalo, New York.

Today Tommy Reid has a ministry that has taken him beyond the building of a church in one locale, beyond denominational walls, to charismatic clinics and seminars held across the world. Now he uniquely exposes his very self to you through the written page. May the truths expressed in *The Exploding Church* explode in your heart, releasing in you a fountain that will flow freely to a thirsty and dying world.

Dr. Paul Younggi Cho, Pastor
Full Gospel Central Church
Seoul, Korea

The future . . . seems to me no unified dream but a mince pie, long in the baking, never quite done.

(E.B. White, *One Man's Meat*)

1

Vision of the Future

I was sitting in the midst of revival.

It was 1962, and Pentecost was sweeping the great Eternal Life Presbyterian Church in Chun-ju, South Korea.

For weeks I had crisscrossed the nation with my father, holding mammoth crusade meetings in five of the great cities of South Korea. God had blessed our services with tremendous miracles of healing and beautiful outpourings of His Holy Spirit. Hundreds of Koreans from every religious background were speaking in unknown tongues and exercising the gifts of the Spirit.

On this particular night I sat on the platform and watched a minister lead the massive congregation in singing. Thousands of Korean faces moved in unison as they sang the lyric: "The Comforter is come, the Comforter is come."

Suddenly my vision began to blur. The congregation faded out; the song leader disappeared. Panic gripped me. I squinted and blinked my eyes, but I could not see!

Then just as suddenly, the faces reappeared. Now they were no longer Korean faces. Instead, the church was filled with a multitude of Caucasian faces. The people were clapping their hands and singing and praising God with thunderous enthusiasm.

I looked at the minister who was leading the song. In the vision I saw him wearing the robes of a Catholic priest.

I realized, somehow, that the vision was a scene from Buffalo, New York—the city of my birth. I was seeing a scene from the future.

Clearly, undeniably, God spoke to my spirit: *Tommy, I will do more for your ministry in Buffalo than I have ever done for you before.*

Instantly the picture vanished. I sat once again in Chun-ju, South Korea—deeply puzzled.

It was no simple promise God had made to me. How could the future possibly be greater than the past? I wasn't even thirty years old, and already I had experienced magnificent success in the ministry. Before coming to Korea, I had co-pastored with my father our denomination's largest church in the Philippines. And throughout my ministry, I had preached to large crowds in tremendous evangelistic crusades all over America and the world. My reputation was rock-solid in the Pentecostal world. My ministry was firmly established, and I was proud of my success.

I put the vision out of my mind. It seemed so silly. Buffalo? There was not a single outstanding church of my denomination in Buffalo. From my standpoint, it was a small-time city.

With a shrug I said to myself, "If this is of God, it will happen."

Silly as it seemed, however, the vision would not let go. After the Korean crusade I headed back to Buffalo, my evangelistic headquarters, and soon I felt compelled to check into the possibility of pastoring there. The denominational leadership mentioned an opening at South Buffalo Tabernacle.

"What would you want to pastor *that* church for?" my stepmother asked. "It's mostly empty seats!"

Her concise analysis was accurate. The tabernacle was a self-satisfied church of about 110 people. "Certainly no trophy," I told myself, "for a spiritual leader of my experience and finesse!"

But one day I cleaned out my garage and loaded my Cadillac with the unwanted junk. Ironically, it was on my way to the dumps that God cleared my perspective and told me to pursue the ministry of the tabernacle.

I candidated before a congregation of thirty-eight people. An inauspicious beginning.

Still, God had promised great things for me in Buffalo, and on that basis I began my work there with a sense of glad anticipation. Somehow—I wasn't sure exactly how—I believed God would make Buffalo the highlight of my career.

I was about to be grievously disappointed.

"Where there is no vision," Proverbs declares, "the people perish" (29:18). The vision is not necessarily a flash of light or a moving picture. Many times it is only a concept, a notion.

Still, God has a divine plan for every ministry in the world. God's desire is for every man's ministry to be successful, for every vision to be fulfilled.

God's vision is the beginning of every man's ministry, regardless of how ego-centered that ministry eventually becomes. The balance is a precarious one. God gives a man a vision of the church he is to start, or the mission program he is to inaugurate, or the media ministry he is to develop, and the man gets excited. Soon what was holy and righteous becomes an ego trip. What was God's becomes man's—and the preacher has slipped from the divine plan into the human. Every spiritual leader battles this syndrome. Even the apostle Paul fought the battle with self, and called himself a "wretched man" for faring so poorly in it.

I suffered from the syndrome too—I had it bad.

But the vision is God's—absolutely. God entrusts it to man, but man cannot alter the vision, no matter how much his human nature interferes.

That night in Korea, when God showed me that church full of Caucasian faces, He established within me His vision for my ministry. In that moment He sealed His promise in my heart.

For seven years my work in Buffalo gasped and faltered. There were many times when all I had to go on was that vision. On some days the promise of God seemed to be an impossible ideal. I did not know I was standing in its way; yet every day I returned to that vision.

The church continued lifeless for seven years. By that time, I was tired. Perhaps my guard finally dropped when the job had worn me out. That's probably how God finally caught me by the spiritual ears and changed the course of my entire ministry.

In the next few months, God was to teach me three startling lessons, illuminating the principles of His Word through a strange and disturbing series of events.

My ministry, as I knew it, was about to come to a complete stop. I would learn what I had never learned in all my years behind the pulpit—the real meaning of the ministry, the real secret of church growth, and the original plan of God for His church. The heavenly Father would weed out my prefabricated notions one by one—building a new perspective, a new mode of ministry, piece by painful piece.

By His own hand, God was about to lay the cornerstone of "the exploding church."

I preached as never sure to preach again,
And as a dying man to dying men.

(Richard Baxter, *Love, Breathing, Thanks, and Praise*)

2

Standing Backwards in the Pulpit

I hope you never heard me back then.

I was the preacher, the pulpiteer, the showman, and I felt that my "show" was one of the best. It is a far cry from my ministry today, but my first sixteen years as a preacher were earmarked by *how well I preached*.

The theme of my denomination for many years has been this Scripture: "Not by might, nor by power, but by my spirit, saith the Lord" (Zech. 4:6). I have quoted it hundreds, perhaps thousands, of times. My files bulge with sermons preached on that single verse. It makes a good slogan for pumping church growth.

I also solidly believed it. I believed that God built His church not by any kind of human strength, but by the moving of His Holy Spirit in the hearts and affairs of men.

But quoting it, preaching it, and believing it never

brought me to the point of practicing it. Zechariah 4:6 never came alive in my actual day-to-day ministry. It was concept, but not concrete.

Indeed, I felt the Spirit's anointing in my messages. I witnessed the results of that anointing as souls were saved and believers were filled with the Holy Spirit.

But my own might and power remained the mainstays of my pulpit ministry. Week after week I concocted my sermons to satisfy my own lust to perform for the people. I prepared my messages through solitary and careful study, packed them full of catchy clichés and fascinating facts. I scrupulously memorized my sermons, as well as the orations of others. I borrowed heavily from the greats—T. Dewitt Talmage, Aimee Semple McPherson, and many others. I geared up for every sermon with one eye on the Scriptures and the other eye on the next audience, hoping they would be held rapt by my stage presence.

Then, as I finished my preparation of each sermon, I would go before God with a last minute, fervent request. "Lord, anoint me in this service," I would pray with grievous sincerity, "so that souls might be saved."

The salvation of lost souls was an honorable motive. My heart, however, had already begged for something else. My attitude at the drawing board had already asked for the applause of men.

Using God's anointing for human gain is a common sin among preachers. The technique works to some extent. God does not let His Word return void. He continued to bless the hearts of my congregation through my sermons. But my reward had already been given to me as I stepped onto the stage and puffed myself up for the performances I so loved. My words flowed; the Spirit did not.

Still I played my part—I knew my job, and I did it right.

With my sermons precise as Swiss clockwork, I saw myself capturing minds, stopping time, chilling flesh. In the tabernacle and the many other places where I spoke across the country, I was dash and vigor and pomp, expounding the great spiritual truths with style and passion and outstanding elocution. I was *the preacher*, and I loved it.

But I felt the creeping, growing void in my spirit as each performance concluded. Even beyond the inevitable emotional letdown that follows almost any public appearance, I felt something profound happening within me. I could feel the smoldering signals of a spiritual ulcer. A sense of unrest enveloped me, and each time I closed a service I heard my hidden self sadly muttering, "God is displeased with me." But I did not know why.

Something was backwards.

Perhaps I was striving for intellectual superiority because the anti-intellectualism of my Pentecostal heritage haunted me. I was raised in the classical Pentecostal tradition long before speaking in tongues had become fashionable. I grew up in fear of being called that most devastating of nicknames: "holy roller."

Now, as a respected member of the worldwide evangelical community, I no longer deserved that degrading label. I still believed in speaking in tongues—but I was careful to call it glossolalia—and in fact I had spoken in tongues myself back in Bible college. But I was by no means a roller of any sort, holy or otherwise. I was not a fanatic; no, sir!

When anyone asked me what I believed, I sidestepped the facts and declared calmly that my doctrine was something like the Southern Baptists. As long as I could, I avoided exposing myself as a "tongues person." It was always a relief to get out from under that Pentecostal cloud and into the drier, safer camp with the famous, respectable, successful Baptists.

"If only we Pentecostals could achieve their stature, their reputation!" I often said to myself.

When the charismatic movement exploded in the early 1970s, I cringed. Here they were, dragging out the dirty linen for all the Christian world to see.

Before long, however, it was vogue to be

Pentecostal. All you had to do was call yourself "charismatic" and you were *in*. Suddenly the liberals, the Catholics, and many others were speaking in tongues!

But now the classical part of my classical Pentecostal upbringing took over. As a devout fundamentalist, I shook a godly fist at those undisciplined spiritual snippets and I challenged their spiritual experience. *My* plan for the church would never permit a practicing Catholic to receive the baptism in the Holy Spirit!

Still, something odd was taking shape all over the world. I could see what looked like God's genuine blessings being poured out on groups of all kinds—from the Greek Orthodox to the conservative Presbyterians. Even in my own corner of Buffalo, the local Catholic priest was leading the worship of more than five hundred enthusiastic Catholics in his weekly charismatic prayer meeting. All of this was happening while I continued sermonizing to my two hundred satisfied saints, lauding our successes and explaining away our failures. Now and then I "took a shot" at that priest from my pulpit, but usually I simply ignored him. He was, after all, not part of my denomination, and he was Catholic to boot—with the robes and the collars, no less.

And the Jesus people, those long-haired,

blue-jeaned revolutionaries, were a disconcerting element in the religious scene of Buffalo. They had just begun to take hold in the area. If there was ever any group that was "of the world," I thought, here they were!

I thought the Full Gospel Business Men were a nuisance in Buffalo too. They were spotlighting some of America's greatest speakers. People told me that their meetings were "sensational" month after month. Of course, I never attended a meeting myself. I didn't agree with their methods. They were competing with me for the Buffalo market. I scoffed at them.

"The Full Gospel Business Men, like the Catholic charismatics and the Jesus people, are mixing with the world," I said to myself and my parishioners. We, on the other hand, were "coming out from among them, praise God!" We were "being separate." Those other guys would let *anybody* into their meetings! "Unhealthy, unwise, unscriptural," I sighed.

"Besides," I rationalized, "crushing the competition is the name of the pastoral game in the church world today." So we bought ourselves a bus, hired a busing pastor, and made plans to buy another bus. For a more sophisticated approach, we also purchased a van. I attended convention after seminar after conference on the methods of Sunday school promotion, use of the media, record-keeping, and administration. We designated thousands of dollars in each annual budget for promotional programs. We produced a daily quarter-hour program on a Christian radio network all across New York State. We drove genuine Indians in genuine Indian costumes through Buffalo in a caravan of convertibles to promote our Sunday school. We dropped printed publicity from balloons. We stuffed the *Buffalo Evening News* with spiffy ads promoting big-name evangelists we had scheduled to fill our pulpit. "IN PERSON! ONE NIGHT ONLY!"

Why? Ostensibly, to reach lost souls with the salvation message. But in reality I was struggling to hold my own parcel of ground and cut into the next guy's turf. Hopefully, I told myself without thinking, I will be able to draw off a few of those neighboring Methodists—or even a couple of those misguided Catholic charismatics—and get them into our camp where they can finally be spiritually fed.

I wanted my church to be the biggest in Buffalo. Biggest is best—this is what I had come to believe in the realm of the spiritual. I had learned well. From the moment I stepped onto campus, my Bible college training focused heavily on success schemes for church growth. This trend has grown since my own campus days. Today the *spiritual* growth of the church is only a third of the fledgling pastor's concern. He has just left a Bible school that has trained him to be equally tenacious in his drive for *numerical* gain and *financial* gain.

Our denominational publications feed this notion by puffing the biggest congregations and the biggest church buildings and the biggest offerings. Outdoing the next fellow—friend and foe alike—has become the highest achievement in many church circles today. Empire-building is the *cause célèbre* of modern Christianity.

Of course, in spite of all my own empire-building, I could still quote that inconspicuous little scriptural commandment about seeking not your own but "another man's wealth." It bothered me a little bit that I couldn't apply that pure a principle to my own life and ministry. I was frankly amazed that it was even in the Scriptures at all. Obviously no one could live up to a standard like that; nobody's motivation was so upright and selfless.

For instance, I would rather have a new Cadillac than see my neighbor drive one into his garage. And the feeling was amplified a little if the neighbor were another pastor. Society told me I had to keep up with the local Joneses, and in fact supersede them. I was on the prowl constantly for a better neighborhood, a finer home, a higher standing in the community. In my personal life, I was certainly not hoping to discover any deeper meaning in that inconspicuous, little, seek-your-neighbor's-wealth directive.

It was the same in my ministry. It was absurd to think of interpreting that principle literally when it came to community church politics. If it were possible, I would have had every person in Buffalo attend my church. I was certainly not going to support a neighboring pastor in any crusade or campaign, particularly if he were not part of my denomination. I was trying to build my church, not fracture it.

Still, the principle of seeking my neighbor's wealth, tucked away in 1 Corinthians 10:24, pricked at me a little from time to time as I chaired staff planning meetings and supervised the creation of new growth schemes—schemes that would succeed only at the expense of the other pastors in town.

My life-trained instincts told me that the numerical growth of my congregation was the greatest single indicator of my own professional success as a minister. I looked forward to the day when I would be able to say, "We have the biggest Sunday school in town. We give more to missions than any other church in the state. We have the biggest church building in the country. More buses than . . . more square feet than . . . more Sunday school classes than . . . a bigger budget than. . . ."

It was a perspective that drove me to push for growth by the sweat of my natural brow.

But even as my staff and I scrupulously constructed program after program—and each time prayed earnestly for God's anointing on our plans—something told me I had it all backwards.

In the long haul, our attendance did increase to a degree. We were able to draw in a few new families by canvassing the neighborhoods with promotional zeal.

But even so, our growth was spastic. Scheduled revivals failed to revive us. The numbers on the tally board fluctuated, and the church remained lifeless.

Seven years saw little growth. I quoted my percentages and made my claims at each denominational convention, but inside I was losing the spirit of the fight.

Perhaps, I mused many times in those long months, the move to Buffalo had been a mistake. Perhaps it was not God's plan for me at all. Perhaps that vision of Buffalo had been only a fluke of my imagination, a momentary mental lapse brought on by some Korean dish.

My reputation as a compelling evangelist had dissolved. And, even though I had used the same promotional techniques that built crowds on the evangelistic circuit, my quest for high marks as a pastor had failed. Who knows how many airplane rides and trips to the Fantasy Island amusement park I gave away in exchange for a little personal evangelism on the part of my parishioners? In spite of all my methods, my church had not exploded.

Instead, somewhere, somehow, God's promise of great things in Buffalo had evaporated.

And come he slow, or come he fast,
It is but Death who comes at last.

(Sir Walter Scott, *Marmion*)

3

Rickshaw with Racing Stripes

The Queen Elizabeth Way stretches forever—or it seemed to the night I was driving between London, Ontario, and Buffalo. My eyelids burned for sleep.

Our church was beginning a building program, so I had to be on hand at the construction site as often as possible. That week, though, I was the featured speaker at a camp meeting at the London fairgrounds. So several late nights found me driving the Q.E.W. back to Buffalo.

The camp meetings were going well; attendance was fair to good. Construction on our church was going well too. But my heart was longing for God. There was a parched feeling in my spirit.

As I fought to stay awake on the highway that night, I began twisting the radio dial, desperate to find some program to keep me from falling asleep at the wheel.

In the midst of all the crackling static, a familiar voice broke through. It was Kathryn Kuhlman, the famous woman of faith, being interviewed by one of Canada's leading radio personalities on a coast-to-coast program.

Although it helped a little to follow their conversation, I still felt myself sagging with fatigue. Then, suddenly, Kathryn said something that cut through my exhaustion and made me sit up straight.

"Every time I go to the platform," she said quietly, "I die a thousand deaths."

I was shaken by the statement. Kathryn Kuhlman? Afraid of ministering in public? In spite of her quiet, sincere manner, the woman may as well have stepped out of the radio and slapped me sharply across the face. Kathryn Kuhlman had appeared before hundreds of thousands of people in person over the space of many years. Her ministry was always beautiful, articulate, and poised. I was shocked to hear this renowned evangelist telling a nationwide audience—so sincerely—that she dreaded every service.

I could not relate to this concept. I had never died even one of those proverbial "thousand deaths." I loved to preach. I thrived on my public ministry. Ascending the steps of a platform was my personal physiological trigger for adrenalin surge. And my ministry had come nowhere close to the stature of

Kathryn Kuhlman's.

So why would she recoil in the pulpit? If she were really sincere—and I believed in my spirit that she was—then her reasoning must be completely alien to mine.

I struggled with this thought as I drove down the expressway. It would not leave me alone. *"I die a thousand deaths."* Somewhere, I said to myself, she must have an insight I don't have. And then I found myself breaking before the Lord, crying out for a fresh injection of His Spirit, a fresh look at the ministry in Buffalo.

"Tommy, I am going to teach you what she meant," I heard God say to me. "Someday you will share her view."

Kathryn Kuhlman's simple, yet complex, statement was to radically change my life. Soon I began an anxious search through the Scriptures. I began to pursue what God had promised—a new view of the ministry, a new perspective on my life's work.

As long as I could remember, Kathryn had said she totally depended on the Holy Spirit in her ministry. She keenly felt her own human inability to meet the needs of her audiences.

This was an inability I did not feel at all. I had a sense of complete adequacy about the abilities of Tommy Reid. Perhaps it was actually a sense of superiority. I felt I could handle the administration of a large parish. I saw myself as an orator. I held the attention and respect of my people.

I looked at Kathryn, then at myself, then back at Kathryn. She had not clenched her fists and strained to achieve success in the ministry. Morcover, she felt she had nothing to offer her audiences. So she had surrendered her entire ministry to God, offering herself up as an empty vessel to be used by the Holy Spirit as He saw fit.

It was the Holy Spirit's work through Kathryn Kuhlman, then, that I had interpreted as a beautiful, poised ministry. Kathryn was not in charge of those services at all. She had nothing to do with the success of her meetings. And she was so yielded to God that she died over and over before every service—knowing that only God's Holy Spirit could salvage the meeting and make something useful of it.

She had surrendered her Isaac. Like Abraham, she had established her belief in the absolute sovereignty of God over her life.

When he laid his only son across the altar of death, Abraham was declaring his absolute selflessness. From that moment on, Abraham considered everything he owned to be the property of God.

Once that transfer of ownership was made, God began blessing Abraham. From that moment on,

Abraham was established forever as the father of Israel. Likewise, as Kathryn Kuhlman turned her entire life and ministry over to God, He began blessing her work in magnificent and miraculous ways. Before long, she became one of history's most successful healing evangelists. But the success was not hers at all—she died a thousand deaths before every service. Instead, God was blessing *His own*.

Kathryn Kuhlman had discovered the eternal principle that *God blesses what He possesses*. Indeed, God blesses *only* what He possesses, whether that be an individual, a family, a church, or a nation. God can bless only that over which He has been made sovereign.

My eyes popped open as the Holy Spirit spoke this principle to my heart for the first time. Whose success was I pursuing in my pulpit? Tommy Reid's. Whose reputation was I promoting in my parish? Tommy Reid's. My ministry was my own, a self-spawned, self-satisfying source of pride. My Isaac was my own ministry. Of course I credited God with giving my ministry to me—just as Abraham knew that Isaac was a gift from God. But I had never given that offspring back to God.

It was no minor idiosyncrasy of Scripture I had violated here. I had crossed a rock-solid principle of God's Word. By ceaseless repetition God has established this pattern for His people: Abraham gave Isaac back, Moses' mother gave Moses back, Hannah gave Samuel back, Jesus gave back His own life, the list goes on and on. In every case, God blessed what He possessed.

As the years of self-centeredness rolled back from my eyes, I realized with a sense of spiritual nausea what I had done to my church. At the heart of the problem, I had indeed made it "my church." South Buffalo Tabernacle (renamed Full Gospel Tabernacle) was mine. The people were *my* people.

But God widened my perspective further. Suddenly I saw that the sickness I had was also evident in churches all around the world. Pastor after pastor had established his claim of ownership on "his" church. Sadly, the situation came clear to me: thousands of ministries are not being blessed as they could be, are not enjoying God's anointing to the fullest, because He has not been made sovereign over them. Pastors have not surrendered their Isaacs to God any more than I had surrendered mine. And God will not bless what He does not possess.

Obviously God is still blessing in the world. The windows of heaven have not been boarded shut because of man's self-centered attitude. But God still works within His established principles, and He is only blessing to the extent to which we are giving up our ministries to Him. As long as we claim ownership of our talents and abilities, our ministerial programs and techniques, our churches and ministries, God's hands are tied.

I was terrified by what I saw in my own church. My performances in the pulpit had been standing between my people and God's blessings. Now I saw the worthlessness of my eloquence. I was designing my sermons as fancy attachments to a half-powered ministry—like painting racing stripes on a rickshaw.

The long hours under my desk lamp now seemed a waste, as I realized I had been striving to be blessed for something not possessed by God. I had been preparing each service by filling myself—instead of emptying myself and allowing the Spirit to shine through me. I was clutching my ministry to myself—(a) unwilling to let it go, (b) unhappy to see it stagnate, and (c) unable to understand how one would solve the other.

It embarrassed me to recall my last-minute prayers over my pat sermon outlines, feverishly asking God to anoint the messages I had so ably and professionally produced. The Holy Spirit showed me, in scene after typical scene, the many ways I had missed the ministerial mark by not surrendering my Isaac.

It was clear to me I would have to make a decision about my ministry. ("My ministry" suddenly seemed like such a carnal phrase!) I knew that the surrender of my Isaac would have to be concrete, not just concept. I knew it meant a change of heart. But I also knew it meant a definitive, actual alteration of my pulpit presentations. Something in my stomach told me I had put on my last performance. The show had closed. From now on, God would be taking over—cuing the lines, arranging the scenes.

But exactly how this change would take place, I could not yet know. God was still not through retraining me. I had two troubling lessons to go.

But felt through all this fleshly dress
Bright shoots of everlastingness.

(Henry Vaughan, *Silex Scintillans*)

4

World with a Broken Heart

God seemed best able to get ahold of me in my car. While driving north on the Niagara extension of the New York State Thruway I was praying. I knew my perception needed to be altered, and at this moment I was praying, "God, show me the world as you see it."

I was ill-prepared for His response to that simple prayer. Just as I passed the Seneca Street ramp, the scenery all around suddenly seemed to fade. Then a large globe appeared in the sky ahead of me. I felt I was flying like an astronaut, viewing the world from outer space.

Two great arms, as if they were the arms of God, reached down from heaven and pulled the world into two pieces, exposing its insides. Inside, I saw a huge, broken heart, bleeding. I remember a deep sadness overwhelming my spirit.

"Son, this is how I see the world," the Spirit of God

said to me gently. "And this is how I want you to see it."

The sight of that broken world became a point of reference for me in the months and years that followed. My own ministry slowly unfolded before me as God brought me back again and again to that world with a broken heart.

What God began to reveal to me was disturbing. I was not ministering to broken hearts. I was not really ministering to people at all. When I looked out at my congregation, I did not see people with needs. If anything, I saw sins, which of course needed forgiving. I saw souls to be saved from sin, numbers to be totaled up at the altar and published in next month's magazine.

I was usually looking at the outer man, rarely at the burdened inner man. I saw the sin, instead of the hurts those sins were causing. I rarely perceived my congregation as people who needed answers to prayer in their lives.

God's Spirit slowly awakened me to the reality of my ministry—and all of my ministerial methods. Before He was done with me, my sermons were only a tiny slice of the problem pie.

The evangelistic quest of the church, obviously, is to see new converts born into the kingdom. I always thought the key word in that concept was *new*. New converts meant new totals on the church books. But as my troubled spirit opened up to the Father's leading, God showed me that the key word is *born*.

I had distorted the birth process.

God's law from the beginning was that the species would produce "after their own kind" (Gen. 1). Man was designed that way. Animals were designed that way. Plants likewise.

What we ignore is the fact that the birth principle is universal and unilateral. God designed everything He created with the birth principle at its foundation. Marriages produce after their own kind. Note the huge percentage of divorcees whose parents were divorced. Governments produce after their own kind. Read the history of Israel, as her people followed the particular spiritual persuasions of her kings.

All of God's creation operates under the birth principle. It is the foundation of every other principle: the principle of seedtime and harvest, the principle of giving and receiving, the principle of sin and death, and on and on.

Churches also operate under the birth principle. I looked at our church's struggle to grow. We could add a family here and there if we really worked at it, but it was hard to keep new families in the fold. They were not prone to grow spiritually and take root in the church. *For some reason.*

The reason is now vividly and painfully clear to

me. A church giving birth to new converts by fleshly means will fill its pews with fleshly converts. Human methodology, humanly conceived, will produce human results. And, as I focused on the outer man, and the numbers of people attending each service, my fleshly motive was reaping a fleshly harvest. Our growth, such as it was, could only be described as human. We had certainly not experienced a supernatural explosion in our church!

A shopworn verse of Scripture took a new meaning: "That which is born of the Spirit is spirit" (John 3:6). Spiritual Christians will be born through spiritual means. Carnal Christians will be born through carnal means. The numbers game might produce numbers—but not revival.

It was a devastating experience to see my church program for the first time in the light of the birth principle. I had taken that approach so widely accepted among pastors and church workers today: "Get them inside any way you can, then let the Holy Spirit take over."

Honorable logic, but faulty in its conception. This theory runs counter to God's birth principle. "That which is born of the Spirit is spirit." This means that which is dragged into the church by man-made gimmickry is man-made—and, like the gimmick, short-lived. "Except the Lord build the house, they labor in vain that build it" (Ps. 127:1).

God has shown me over and over, in every area of my ministry, how the arms of flesh have interfered with the building of His church. The contests, the parades, the giveways—all the publicity stunts—have been stripped of their earthly glamor and exposed to the eye of faith.

God said, "I will build my church," but in many cases the pastor has chosen to do it for Him. At the tabernacle we were deeply involved in media advertising—through radio, newspapers, and direct mail. These efforts consumed a large percentage of our budget every month—to keep the crowds coming in. God began showing me the folly of all fleshly effort.

Still, I had no immediate alternatives. What does a minister do if he can't advertise? How do you draw new people without promotion? How do you keep the dollars flowing in without faithful pumping?

"If I don't do any of that," I pleaded helplessly with God, "I don't know what to do!"

I got no immediate answers—only the nagging realities. All the truths spinning from God's birth principle kept gnawing at me. If I was to have an exploding church, it would happen because I searched the Scriptures and opened my spirit to God's.

As the days rolled on, I developed a sort of spiritual skepticism. I began taking a long, hard look not only at my own church but at the modern church as a whole. Soon I was convinced that we had to reexamine all of our methods: our sermons, our growth campaigns, even our form of worship.

Some of our worship services are completely earthbound, based almost entirely on fleshly construction. The service is often designed to make an emotional impact and produce an emotional response. The product of such a service is an emotionally motivated Christian.

I deeply love to praise the Lord, but whooping it up to the tune of "Since Jesus Came into My Heart" does not necessarily qualify as genuine worship. The Bible tells us to live in the Spirit and pray in the Spirit, but somehow we tend to automatically equate the moving of the Spirit with a noisy production.

Since God began dealing with me about my worship services, I have discovered that a congregation can move into true spiritual worship without being told to raise their hands and without any musical backup at all. In many Pentecostal churches today, once the drum stops beating and the organ stops throbbing and the volume of the service dies down, the emotionally motivated Christian goes into an emotional low, which he usually identifies mistakenly as a spiritual low. It is a vicious but common syndrome—one I witnessed, and indeed created, under my own ministry for many years.

Even the more recently fashionable charismatic worship, which basically has no form, tends to become a form of its own. The singing in the Spirit, the quiet praising of the Lord—this is not the ultimate way to worship either. We have merely moved into a form more fitting with the times—leaving behind the rowdy circus days of P.T. Barnum and entering the low-key era of Johnny Carson and talk shows.

The church needs to remind itself constantly that it is striving for heavenly worship—to worship God on earth as we will someday worship Him in heaven. This means we can never attach ourselves to any form of worship without being consistently open to the leading of the Holy Spirit. The church must be in a state of continual renewal.

Sermons and worship services both suffer at our human hands; but even more pervasive in the church today is the fleshliness of evangelism. I glibly justified every high-pressure growth campaign on the solid foundation of the Great Commission: "Go ye into all the world, and preach the gospel to every creature" (Mark 16:15). But in truth, our Sunday school programs seldom reflected the spirit of Christ's solemn directive. Aside from my desire to get a greater share of recognition in the big Christian magazines, I was prodding people into my church in a spirit of competition with the neighboring pastors. Even nearby churches of my own denomination were adversaries in this "numbers game."

As I reached deeper and deeper into the mass-media pot, I found that promotion feeds on itself and creates even more distortion of the Great Commission. Media advertising cost us huge amounts of money, which inflated our financial need at offering time, which inflated our need for a bigger congregation, which inflated our need for promotion, *ad infinitum.*

Spiritual converts are birthed only by true spiritual methodology. The first 3,000 converts in the book of Acts were conceived in the hearts of the 120 in the Upper Room. The amazed crowd gathered because they saw the Spirit being poured out on the 120—not because they expected fisherman Peter to preach a memorable message or because they had been hooked by some flashy newspaper ad. God's spiritual birth process was at work, and God showed me that this process was plainly not at work in my own ministry—nor in many others.

Ask many ministers how they justify their huge outlay of time and attention and money for the sake of getting more money. Many will tell you what I would have told you in defense of my own small outreach in Buffalo: "Dollars mean souls." It has almost become the modern church's credo. It is simply another version of "Get them inside any way you can, then let the Holy Spirit take over."

But so often this attention to dollars warps the spiritual effectiveness of both the man and his ministry. By the time he has come to believe that dollars do indeed mean souls (in much the same way that I once believed sermons meant souls, without regard for the creativity of the Holy Spirit), he already has serious perspective problems. Beyond that, the new convert then finds himself not at a spiritual feeding ground but rather in a self-perpetuating fund-raising campaign, feeding a monster that eats only to live and lives only to eat.

God's call in my own life was clear. He had shown me specifically the fleshliness of my sermons, of my services, of my schemes for church growth. I barely knew how to react. I could hardly cancel my newspaper ads or my radio outreach or my plans for a television ministry. I couldn't realistically stop preaching sermons, or suddenly revamp the order of worship in my church.

And yet, with God's birth principle so badly battered and staring me in the face, those far-fetched options seemed to be the only solution.

. . . Gonna find me some peace of mind
And if that peace of mind won't stay
I'm gonna find myself a better way
And if that better way ain't so
I'll ride with the tide and go with the flow.
(Inez and Charlie Foxx, "Mockingbird")

5

Go with the Flow

The third lesson—the most jarring one—was introduced in relative calm.

I was scheduled to hold meetings for the Christian Centre in Toronto, but a long string of obstacles stood in the way of the plan. We managed to avoid cancellation and the meetings began. As I settled down and settled in, I felt that the services represented only a secondary purpose for my trip to Toronto.

The meetings were going well, but after the service one evening, I could not sleep. It was deep night. I got out of bed, donned my robe and slippers, and padded to the balcony of the high-rise apartment where I was staying.

It was cold and crisp and the city of Toronto spread out before me. There was no vision, no supernatural change of scenery. But this third message from God was to cut more deeply into the heart of my ministry than any other.

"Never again ask me to anoint your ministry," God said as I shivered on that balcony. "From now on, Tommy, *become part of what I am doing.*"

I was dumbfounded. I thought I was already part of what God was doing. My program, my sermons, my music, my media outreaches.

And there God illuminated the problem. I was making Him part of what I was doing. I was working counter to His birth principle.

God began to peel back the blinders, to let me see what was really happening in Buffalo. That bothersome Catholic priest down the street—the charismatic I had so scrupulously avoided because of my denominational ties—was the man in town whom God was blessing abundantly. The Full Gospel Business Men, meeting in the "unchurchly" Holiday Inn, were enjoying wave after wave of the Holy Spirit's power. Even the Jesus people were in revival. God was teaching me by default what every preacher must learn before he can be a spiritual success: *We must become part of what God is doing in the world.*

I was surprised to find I had cut myself off from the worldwide flow of God's Spirit. For fear of contaminating my church, I had declared a hands-off policy toward any group outside my denomination—regardless of the Spirit's leading. I had been putting God in a box, presuming that His Holy Spirit would minister exclusively to my denomination.

Meanwhile, refusing to be denied, the Spirit had flowed freely where men and women of God were willing to give up their preconceived notions and freely worship Him. The Catholic charismatics, the Full Gospel Business Men, the Jesus people, and other groups in Buffalo were actually succeeding spiritually, while I struggled to promote my own nervous act across town.

This principle, I soon realized, has been true all through church history. The people who refused to flow with the Martin Luthers, the John Wesleys, the William Booths, and other revivalists of their day went into spiritual decay. Those who flowed in the stream of renewal, however, became alive and healthy, vital forces in church history.

I had already observed the same principle during my own lifetime. Those churches in my denomination that had participated in the great healing revivals of the 1950s—cooperating with ministers such as Oral Roberts—began to grow by great strides. Meanwhile, many of the churches that refused to flow with the stream of the Spirit struggled to break even.

Even in the present, I observed, the churches that

were flowing in the charismatic dimension were growing. Those who opposed it were continuing to struggle.

With a red face I had to admit to myself that I had become as stiff-necked as many of my predecessors. I believed in the same gifts of the Spirit as my charismatic neighbors, but as a status-quo-oriented, denominational Pentecostal, I lacked their freshness and enthusiasm. And this freshness was theirs because they were flowing with God.

Then, like a flower blooming, that inconspicuous little verse gradually unfolded before me: "Let no man seek his own, but every man another's wealth" (1 Cor. 10:24). My empire-building ran exactly counter to God's law.

As the Word began to cut deep into my spiritual character, it laid bare my foundational motivation. It was wrong, impure, unscriptural. I was not concerned with the other minister's gain. I was indeed concerned only with my own. Furthermore, I was pursuing my own church's success at the expense of the others!

I should have known. I had no excuse for missing that beautiful line from Jesus' Sermon on the Mount: "Blessed are the pure in heart" (Matt. 5:8). It reads so passively in the King James Version; yet its message is pungent: *The pure in heart are the ones who will be blessed.*

Christian work is generally accomplished with something less than pure motivation. I saw the black spots on my own heart, but the disease is rampant all through the Christian world. We expend much of our labor under the guise of a burden for souls, when in reality we are laboring under a burden of reputation, a desire for success in the eyes of man, a hunger for the biggest piece of the parish pie.

After all, we tell ourselves, the early church was numerically successful, and that fact must justify the quest for large congregations. But when God strips us down to our motives, we have not come close to a concern for the other man's wealth. I was there; I saw my selfish motives burn up the transmission of my church. And hundreds of churches are racing their engines to no avail as their pastors seek success via impure motivation just as I did.

It is an uphill drag race anyway. Everything the churchman reads, every test he studies, tells him how to get and then foster the success drive. Our spirituality is monitored by attendance tallies, in bricks and shingles. If a man has the largest building, or the most people in Sunday school, or the biggest budget, or the highest missionary offering, he is proclaimed a success.

But this is not God's monitor for success. God ranks His churchmen by how *little* of themselves they project into God's work, by how freely His Spirit is allowed to work through them. *Selflessness equals spiritual success in God's plan for His church.*

I realized that selflessness was the missing ingredient in my ministry recipe—which explained why the taste of success was also missing.

Suddenly in my mind's eye the promotional schemes, the pastoral performances, and the denominational barriers all disappeared together in a single flash. God had commanded me to become part of what He was doing—which left no place for me to build an empire of my own. Pumping and promoting my own ministry was not necessary—and in fact not right. Likewise for performing my sermons in the pulpit for the praise of men, and for isolating my church from the rest of the Pentecostal community.

I had been rigidly defensive toward my neighboring ministers. Now God showed me that the pure motivation He required was more than a mouthful of trite phrases—pure motivation is really expressed in how I feel about the other man.

I discovered that God has an unusual yardstick for measuring success. My success is measured in proportion to the purity of my motives. My motives are measured in proportion to my feelings about my neighboring minister's growth. It is easy to pursue your own growth. How willing are you to pursue your neighbor's growth?

That charismatic Catholic priest was a part of God's kingdom—just like me—a member of the body of Christ. Now, to my amazement, God was telling me to make that priest's success a higher priority than my own! The Tommy Reid Empire I had been trying to build was no longer to be of any consequence to me. The revelation was chilling: *Just as giving oneself to other members in the home is God's ideal, so giving of oneself to other members in the body of Christ—across denominational lines—is also God's ideal.*

Selflessness. It stuck in my throat. It was a bone I had never chewed before.

My first reaction was to clutch at my empire. It was hard-earned, after all, and of great sentimental value to me, if not a source of immense pride and pleasure. I had built it!

Then God played back for me a spooky scene out of the Old Testament. The great King Nebuchadnezzar was strutting through his palace shouting, "Is not this great Babylon, that I have built . . . by the might of my power, and for the honor of my majesty?" (Dan. 4:30). God sent Nebuchadnezzar scampering into the fields like a beast, to eat grass like an ox and grow a scraggly head of hair and claw-like fingernails.

I shuddered. I too had strutted about my palace, declaring the magnificence of my creation. It had never happened overtly or consciously; yet it had happened in my heart over and over, as I thrilled to see what I was accomplishing for God.

But God only blesses what He possesses. When a pastor becomes an empire-builder, he no longer goes with God's flow. Instead, whether he realizes it fully or not, he is trying to adjust the flow of God's Spirit to cover his own territory. Now that God was opening my eyes, I could see how hopeless a task this was. No scrawny desert-dweller ever irrigated his garden by changing the course of the Rio Grande.

My sermons, I saw, were not going with the flow. I was acting and orating and sniping at my fellow Christians along the way.

My growth campaigns were not going with the flow. They were an artificial flood tide. I had created my own flow.

My church was not going with the flow, because I had wrapped up its activities and its attentions in my empire. We had built a fleshly palace and merely painted it with a coat of God's anointing—oblivious to the *river* of anointing flowing fast and free through town!

But how was I to make this exciting concept concrete? Going with the flow—becoming part of what God was doing in Buffalo—would mean putting myself on an even keel with other ministering brethren in the area. It would mean rejoicing as I lost families to a new and flourishing work across town, just as if that pastor were my co-pastor.

In fact, I would have to go even further to fulfill the scriptural command to "seek" my neighbor's wealth. I must actively, aggressively encourage the progress of my neighbor's church. I must pray for the success of the man who had been my rival. I must help him to reap abundantly in the kingdom harvest.

What was God leading me to? Sending my people to other churches? I could see the dismal end of my career lying before me, all my parishioners scattered among Buffalo's churches. Where did God draw the line? How much of my neighbor's wealth had to come out of my pocket?

I felt the burden of God's challenge. I felt compelled to try. Some of the Spirit's promptings seemed outlandish, but after seven unfruitful years in Buffalo I was ready to take a spiritual gamble.

As I moved ahead, I would collide not only with many people inside and outside the church, but with my own timid spirit as well. Before long, the challenge of the exploding church would place my entire ministry in jeopardy.

The crushing decisions still lay ahead. So did the grandest adventure of my life.

My true-love hath my heart, and I have his,
  By just exchange one for the other given:
I hold his dear, and mine he cannot miss,
There never was a better bargain driven.

(Sir Philip Sidney, *The Arcadia*)

6

Hobo Midas

An ultimatum from my people finally set everything in motion.

The tabernacle had hosted a huge number of special speakers and crusades in the past year or more. The congregation was specialed out. Resentment was beginning to run high, and eventually the board of deacons asked me quite sternly, on behalf of the congregation, not to call in any more special speakers or singers for a period of at least six months. I agreed. I was specialed out too.

But within days of my experience in Toronto, when God told me to become part of what He was doing, I received a phone call. The wife of the president of the local Full Gospel Business Men's chapter wanted to know if I would have two musical ministers, a married couple, conduct a service in our church on an upcoming Sunday morning. The couple was being sponsored by the Full Gospel Business Men, and they were scheduled to start a week of services with the Catholic charismatics on that same Sunday evening. They needed a Sunday morning service to help them financially.

I thought back to that night in Toronto: "Become part of what I am doing."

To say yes made no sense. Not only had my congregation given me an ultimatum, but these two singers were part of the "new left movement" in church music, which at the time was far from popular in the mainline Pentecostal churches.

"This is crazy," I told myself. What if I invited them and the board asked for my resignation? I was risking my pastoral position for two hippie-type Jesus people—sponsored by the rival Full Gospel Business Men—with a Catholic connection, yet!

Besides, I would be risking a potential inheritance if I lost the church. An aunt of mine had given the church its property at my own special request. And an adjoining piece of land was likely to become mine by way of her last will and testament. I could imagine my embarrassment at being forced to leave my pastorate after asking my aunt for the highly valuable property she had already given. That piece of ground had represented most of her total worth. I felt I owed it to her to stay put for all of these reasons —and even more so, because she was still living adjacent to the church, on the very property that was to be mine someday. And, in fact, I owed it to myself to stay, because I knew if I ever left the church my aunt would never will me anything at all.

But the voice of God was clear and strong: "Seek your neighbor's wealth. Become part of what I am doing. Go with the flow. Surrender your Isaac. Give me your church. Turn its entire direction over to me—regardless of your vested interest, regardless of your human reasoning, regardless of your deacons' ultimatums. Right now it's all yours. Surrender it all. Make it mine."

I hemmed and hawed. "It's foolhardy for a pastor to cross his board," I told myself—especially since the board had the backing of the whole congregation. It was also risky to rub elbows with that Catholic charismatic crowd. My denominational leadership was likely to slap my wrists. Two left-wing singers weren't worth the risk to my reputation, salary, and inheritance.

The arguments tumbled around inside my head. How can I obey the voice of God and yet disobey the voice of my church board? How can I justify jeopardizing my relationship with my aunt, after her generosity to the church? Hadn't God given me my intellect for making rational decisions? Yes. If I invited these singers, would this qualify as a rational decision? No. Somehow this problem had never come up in any class at Bible college.

Gently the Holy Spirit held firm. God was putting me to the test. Was it *my* church, or *His* church? Could I cross the Jordan on faith? Would I lay my Isaac on the altar?

I did not yet realize that I was facing a larger question than any of these. I was facing the question of covenant.

One of today's most widespread problems—facing churchmen and laymen alike—is that we ignore the broad principles of the Bible. This happens in some cases, because modern attitudes have shortcircuited these principles. In other cases it occurs because the principles are so much a part of the Scriptures themselves that we overlook them.

One such principle is the covenant relationship. It is somehow not in vogue today to refer to the covenant relationship between God and man—as if it were a trite phrase that went out of style with seamed nylon stockings. Neither is it a widely recognized principle of Scripture. The covenant appears so frequently, and is so much a part of everything in the Bible, that it is perhaps subtle. But the covenant relationship is the principle that revolutionized my ministry—and caused the church I pastor to become an exploding church.

The covenant relationship is actually the theme of

the Bible itself—the story of a beautiful exchange between two individuals, God and man.

Exchange is the heart of the covenant. Whenever two men made a covenant in the days of the Old Testament, they always exchanged three things: garments, weapons, and girdles.

A man's garments represented his wealth. By exchanging their garments, two covenant-makers were saying, "My riches are yours. All that I have is yours."

God entered into a covenant relationship with man through Abraham. Each said to the other, "All that I have is yours."

God, of course, had more to offer. He promised Abraham a spacious land, and this assurance: "And I will make of thee a great nation, and I will bless thee, and make thy name great; and thou shalt be a blessing" (Exod. 12:2).

But to fulfill the covenant, Abraham had to give everything he had too. First God asked him to give up his business in Haran and move to Palestine. In Palestine he lost everything through famine and had to move to Egypt for survival. Then God asked him to give up the riches of Egypt, and He pointed Abraham back to Palestine once again. Three times God asked Abraham for his riches.

The second aspect of the covenant was the exchange of weapons, symbolizing strength. When two men entered into a covenant, they unsheathed their swords and exchanged them. When God made a covenant with man, He promised to be man's strength.

All through the Scriptures, God fights for His people. "A thousand shall fall at thy side, and ten thousand at thy right hand; but it shall not come nigh thee" (Ps. 91:7). Man, in turn, promises to give his strength back to God, even though his energy is puny in comparison. Still, this giving of strength is the heart of Christian service.

But the covenant relationship actually rises and falls on the third part of the covenant: the exchange of girdles. The girdle symbolizes the very life of the individual.

God had little need of man's wealth. He had little need of man's strength. Everything man had to offer had already been given him by God.

But along with everything else God gave man, He gave us a free will. Our choices, unlike any other part of us, are truly our own. We can choose to give our lives to God, or we can choose to withhold our lives from Him and live for ourselves. God created man out of a craving for communication, but He does not force us to commune with Him. The heavenly Father loves for His creation to love Him, and on that basis He offered mankind the life covenant: *God would give man His life if man would give God his life.*

When Abraham entered into the covenant with the Creator, he became an extension of God's very life. God gave Abraham a seed, a lineage, and from that lineage came forth an entire people.

Before the covenant, Abraham was as good as dead. Without a son, without a seed, Abraham had no hope of perpetuating himself. Abraham had no life without Isaac, but God promised him, *I will make you alive*.

Abraham was doubtful at first. So was Sarah. They were nearly a hundred years old. They knew the realities. But God was saying, "I have a covenant with you. I will give you life."

And He gave them Isaac.

Still, the covenant relies on *exchange*. Two individuals must exchange their girdles. The covenant revolves around the question, "Do our lives really belong to each other?"

God tested the covenant, to see if Abraham's life really belonged to God. He took Abraham to the mountain and asked him the covenant question: "Does your Isaac really belong to me?"

It is a question every pastor must face. I faced it in my own ministry. I had steadfastly resisted the surrender of my Isaac. My ministry was *mine*.

It was as if I were a hobo, hopelessly bankrupt, and I married a beautiful girl, perhaps the daughter of King Midas, a girl with fabulous wealth. The first two parts of the marriage covenant are simple: the hobo gives her whatever money he has and whatever strength he has. Since he has no money, and therefore no power, it's simple for him to pay up.

The woman in turn gives him endless wealth, and thereby the strength to get out of his hopeless condition. She gives him a life of luxury and political clout to boot.

But suddenly the hobo is no longer a hobo. He has tapped the wealth of Midas. He has parlayed his wife's money and his wife's clout into wealth and clout of his own. He is *independently successful*. He no longer needs his wife's money, let alone her political connections and power.

And the former hobo is no longer willing to maintain the third part of the covenant. His life is his own now. He does not want to give it up to anyone.

Abraham was there. He had become independently wealthy, he was living on his own land, he had a son who could father his grandchildren and give him life. Abraham no longer needed God.

But God and Abraham were in covenant, and God asked the covenant question: "Is your Isaac really mine? Are we still in covenant together? Do our lives really belong to each other?"

I was there too. I had come to that point, to the crisis of the covenant. Was my Isaac my own, or God's?

Every pastor must arrive there as well. Every preacher must come to the crisis of the covenant. He must decide the covenant question: Is my Isaac my own? Am I willing to give everything I have—my ministry, my church, my reputation, my very life—in exchange for the life God has given me?

Even the great men of God must face the covenant question. Many of today's most prominent ministers have grown wealthy and famous because of what God has given them. God asks every one of them—even after they have come to the place of independence—"Is your Isaac your own? Will you truly give me everything you have? Will you rely entirely on me? *Are we still in covenant?*"

A preacher can preach without the anointing of the Holy Spirit. A minister can run a huge organization without the anointing of the Holy Spirit. A pastor can keep on working for God by rote memory, completely void of dependence on God. God will not let His Word return void, and the people sitting under that ministry can continue being blessed. But still God asks that preacher the covenant question: Is your Isaac your own?

A church never explodes until its pastor has surrendered his Isaac. A church never explodes until its pastor has entered into a covenant relationship with God, until he has given up his wealth, his strength, and his very life to God.

It was many days before my inner self was willing to go that far. I felt the pressure squeezing in on me. I wanted to please my aunt. I wanted to please my deacons. I wanted to please my congregation. I wanted to keep my distance with the Catholics, the Full Gospel Business Men, the Jesus people. *I wanted to preserve what I had.*

But finally, exhausted by the internal wrestling match, I prayed, "Lord, even if I die bankrupt and despised—even if I lose my church, my position, my entire ministry—I give it all to you."

Perhaps the scene sounds romantic in a way—the tough pastor softens up. But there was no glee at the moment. I had laid my Isaac naked on the altar. And I expected a messy finish.

Growth is the only evidence of life.

(John Henry, Cardinal Newman,
Apologia pro Vita Sua)

7

Explosion

Faith in God does not necessarily pay off instantly. In this case, from my nervous perspective, the immediate results were horrible.

The sanctuary was amply tense as the two singers walked to the pulpit. But I had not been warned about their third wheel—an elderly evangelist who came with the package.

The congregation sat in stony silence. I could feel their bitterness almost vibrating toward me. I had broken my promise.

I could think of a dozen biblical characters who had stood in the face of opposition to fulfill God's plan. None of them, however, were holding my hand as I faced my angry church at that moment.

As the service began, the whole decision-making process kept reeling through my mind. I had never before defied the wishes of my people. In the natural I knew I was wrong. But in the spiritual sense I knew God had spoken to me. My Isaac was His. We were in covenant.

The couple sang. It might have been a pleasant surprise to find them less "new left" and more middle-of-the-road than I had expected. But no—nothing took the edge off the situation that morning. Everything was almost as awkward and embarrassing and tense as I had expected. At one point the woman even walked down the aisle and began singing in tongues.

The singers presented a full-length program of avant-garde Jesus music. Then the elderly evangelist stood up to preach.

I shuddered. We were going to miss our traditional noon dismissal. I envisioned burning pot roasts and fuming housewives.

Still, the Holy Spirit had been unleashed before the service ever began. At the moment I surrendered my church to God, the Holy Spirit became free to move in and begin flowing.

As I sat there cringing inside, the evangelist's strong Old Testament preaching was somehow warming up the cool parishioners. As he opened up the Scriptures, the people began responding to the flow of the Spirit—slowly at first, then more and more openly. I watched as the Holy Spirit took control of hearts and minds.

By the end of the service, the Spirit had free reign throughout the sanctuary, and God's blessings were pouring forth beautifully. The emotional and psychological and spiritual barriers had begun to dissolve.

"Go with the flow," the Spirit reminded me. "Become part of what I am doing. Seek your neighbor's wealth. Surrender your Isaac."

As I sat watching my congregation weeping and praising God around the altar, I made a decision to follow the Spirit's leading specifically. At the meeting's end, I announced that we were canceling all of our services at the tabernacle for the rest of the week to join these three ministers in their meetings at the Catholic church. It was a radical and abrupt departure for a classical Pentecostal, but God's time had come.

We had witnessed only the first spark of the imminent explosion.

For the first time I saw firsthand the charismatic Catholics I had denounced from my pulpit. In their midst, along with members of my own church, I witnessed their worship—and discovered to my surprise that it was entirely genuine. The same Holy Spirit I had boxed up in my own denomination was sweeping like a raging fire through this Catholic group! All the ingredients were present—I saw altar calls right out of the brush arbor days, hundreds responding to the clear-cut call for a born-again experience.

For the first time, I felt a surging sense of being a part of what the Holy Spirit was doing on the face of the earth.

But what seemed a quirk at the time turned out to be a decision of spectacular impact. At the end of the week, the Catholic priest announced that he was shutting down his Sunday evening prayer meeting so his group could join us at the tabernacle.

Until then, we had about 150 people attending our Sunday night service each week. Suddenly the church boomed; our 350-seat sanctuary clogged with 390 people—more than half of them Catholics—in the first week. We held a second service that night and another 250 attended.

The people at the tabernacle were startled, skeptical, and disgruntled. Many had settled into certain seats for years, and now they found they had to arrive an hour early to claim their favorite spots. Many of the Catholic women wore slacks to church, while the tabernacle people still frowned on the practice. Many of the newcomers were smokers. All of this left many of our people aghast.

The deacons were somewhat put off too. I had crossed them—and now look what had happened to our church! I sensed that a few of the men were deeply angry.

But the Holy Spirit was flowing freely. I had taken my hands off the church. It was God's.

And God began to work swiftly among the deacons. Art Shell, then pastoring in Clearwater, Florida, was scheduled to speak at our church within a matter of days. Without knowing why, Shell felt God distinctly leading him to preach one of his oldest sermons, "Praying for Your Pastor." He dutifully dug it out of his files and dusted it off.

As Shell concluded his sermon, he asked the deacons to gather around me and pray for me. It was a grueling moment for a couple of the men, but the Holy Spirit had broken through. As each man joined me at the front of the sanctuary and we began to pray together, I could feel our hearts uniting in a new oneness of spirit. That time of prayer signaled the beginning of a new era of cooperation and love between the board and me.

It wasn't long before the same breaking and shaping process had opened the hearts of our people to the newcomers from the Catholic church. In the weeks and months that followed, God's Spirit beautifully knit the two peoples together. Weaker Christians were coached and supported by the veteran believers. Lines of communication, once deliberately clogged, now opened as two religious cultures came together. As we opened our hearts to our spiritual brothers and sisters in the city, we found spiritually hungry families flocking through our doors.

Over and over I saw that original vision—the Catholic priest leading songs—and more and more I saw that vision unfolding in reality before me.

We began reaching out to join hands with the Full Gospel Business Men and other charismatic groups in Buffalo as well. Three of the Full Gospel Business Men's chapter presidents began attending the tabernacle.

Every step was an enriching experience for our church. Isolationism had not kept the purity in—it had kept the flow of God's Spirit out.

And even holding two Sunday evening services proved futile. Before long we were forced to build a larger sanctuary on the property.

In the midst of all this came another prompting from God. The covenant would require more—or, to be more accurate, less.

"Surrender your publicity campaigns," God said to me. "Surrender your weekly newspaper ads, your daily radio programs. They are all yours, not mine."

I knew the principles—publicity is integral to church growth. Every church growth manual ever published includes that precept. To my fundamentalist mind-set, it was absolute, universal law.

But God wanted me to let it go, suicidal as it

seemed. I felt Him challenging me to surrender my Isaac. Abraham must have felt the same confusion; God had promised him an offspring, then He asked Abraham to give back the one and only fulfillment of that promise!

As I listened to the Spirit's leading, He cut deeper and deeper into the promotional package I had so carefully and proudly assembled for my church: "Surrender your television plans. Surrender your plans to extend your bus ministry. These too were born of the flesh. They're yours, not mine. Surrender all your Sunday school goals, your promotional gimmicks. Lay them all on the altar."

I hesitated.

"I will build my church," the Spirit reminded me.

In a single sweep, I canceled my radio contracts, shut down plans for a television ministry, stopped the weekly newspaper ad, canceled plans to enlarge our busing outreach, collapsed our latest promotional campaign, and watched with keen interest as the future continued to unfold explosively.

By now the congregation was homogeneous. They had built the new building together— Catholics and Protestants alike—and as a single people they were proud of the beautiful new edifice.

But just as unity prevailed, it was challenged. We were on the verge of moving into the new facility when the local Jesus people came to my office and asked if they could hold their services somewhere in our complex. They had 250 counter-culture Christians, and they needed a place to worship together.

It was a startling development, but God reminded me: "Go with the flow. Become part of what I am doing. Surrender your Isaac. I will build my church."

Our old sanctuary was just right for this new congregation, so I turned it over to them.

The Jesus people didn't stay put, however. Well over half of them were immediately absorbed into our congregation, drawn by the influence of the Holy Spirit in our services. The parishioners watched in something akin to shock as 150 barefoot, blue-jeaned, long-haired young people flocked into our *regular* Sunday worship services.

The problem was no longer as simple as slacks and cigarettes. Now the confused congregation was faced with a crowd who spoke another language altogether. *Like, their heads were into a different thing, man.*

But once again the Holy Spirit ministered love and tolerance and openness to both the congregation and its new subset. In a short time our people were discovering a commonality in the Spirit with the newcomers—not to mention the fact that many of these Jesus people were actually the children of prominent professional and business people and other respected community figures. The two groups became one in worship, one in fellowship, one in Christ's love.*

As the Holy Spirit worked among the congregation, He also continued to work in me. One day, before long, I realized my preaching was sinful. It was a work of man, styled with enticing words, going against God's plan for His vessels.

So I stopped preaching.

Instead, I decided to go with the flow. I laid my preacher's pride on the altar and surrendered my sermons to God. I stopped asking Him to anoint my words. Instead I asked Him to use me any way He wanted in building His kingdom.

I hardly knew what I was asking.

Like cool, running water, my ministry began to flow with the Spirit. The Saturday night struggles to get God's anointing suddenly vanished. Instead of

---

* Even though we shared our entire facility with the Jesus people, they came to us as a separate entity, and they continued to hold their own meetings in our old sanctuary even though many of them were also involved with the church. The Jesus people had their own elders, their own treasury, their own schedule. Over the years, however, many of their elders have also become elders in the tabernacle itself, and the Jesus people are now being assimilated into the tabernacle structure as a ministry of the church. It has not been a legislated change, but rather a move of the Spirit—as God has been allowed to work in His own way and on His own schedule.

spending long hours piecing together a treatise for every service, I began to spend all week praying in the Spirit and singing in the Spirit and reading God's Word under the inspiration of the Spirit.

Services became a delight, where once they had been a demand. I could get up on Sunday morning after a long Saturday night rest and find that God's message was already flowing from my innermost being.

Sermons would no longer suffice. I must *minister*. I must stand as an empty vessel through whom the Holy Spirit could flow.

My sermons became sharing talks, and I soon discovered I was sharing the same things with the believers of Buffalo that men of God were sharing with the believers in dozens of other places. We had been getting our sermons out of the same Book all along, but now we were flowing together in the stream of God's Spirit.

The old emotional ebb and flow became a constant, thrilling pulse. It is tremendously exciting to bear the message of God that is flowing through His entire body.

The anointing is no longer something we pray for—it is something we flow in. As we dismantle our personal empires and become part of what God is doing, the anointing flows freely, because we are going with God's flow.

The growth of the church has never stopped. God continues to send new families into our midst every week.

No circus-like newspaper ad has brought the explosion of growth. No parade or promise of an airplane ride, no personality in the pulpit draws families into our church today. More and more, people are coming to the tabernacle because they are led by the Spirit. Our church has nothing else to offer!

When the pastor and the board and the congregation fully recognized God as the sovereign head of the church, then God stepped in and took over direct control of the operation of the church. And He is a God who never does anything poorly.

I was ignoring every administrative rule of thumb ever taught in Bible college. The results, however, were positively inspiring. What I had tried—and failed—to do in my own strength now came to pass beautifully. Attendance boomed. Giving doubled, tripled, and quadrupled. Our congregation began to represent a complete cross-section of society.

One of the most remarkable results of going with the flow was the change in the quality of our converts. I had never thought in terms of convert quality before, and indeed the term may have an insidious ring, particularly in light of the truth that Christ's blood covers all manner of sin with equal and total redemption.

Still, I watched as the Holy Spirit began to control more and more of our program, and I saw the real operation of John 3:6: "That which is born of the Spirit is spirit." When new people give their hearts to Christ at our altar, I find that they root themselves in the Word much more quickly, much more solidly than the converts from our old promotional campaigns. These Christians are being birthed by the process of the Spirit—God's birth principle—and as a result they are truly *spiritual* men and women.

So often in the modern church, growth and fallout arrive hand in hand. The converts who ride in on the emotional tidal wave are apt to drift out with the same tide. For years I found it hard to hang onto families who came into our fellowship. They either drifted away from the Lord because I had drawn them in by the fleshly arm of promotion—or they longed for deeper spiritual things which my high-powered sermonizing did not minister to them.

Now, as God was allowed to build His church, my sermons ministered in the Spirit's flow—that same flow that is sweeping charismatic and Pentecostal churches all over the earth. And the new Christians entering our midst have been prepared and drawn by God's own Spirit; they are already seeking for that genuine spiritual flow when they walk through our doors. The old build-up-and-fallout syndrome has long disappeared.

At the same time I shocked many pastors in my denomination by sending some of the newer families back to their former churches across town. Many of our people had been pulled into our church as I actively sought out new people from among the neighborhoods where other Spirit-filled and Bible-believing churches were already ministering. Those churches, I reasoned, were not part of my denomination; so they were the competition. I consistently challenged their ministries by laying hold of the people in their care.

Now I saw the sinfulness of that attitude. God had told me to let Him build His church, and if I wanted to promote at all it should be to help the other guy. "Let no man seek his own, but every man another's wealth." My denomination, He showed me, has no corner on the ministerial market.

Furthermore, as people were spiritually revitalized by the move of the Holy Spirit in our church, I was anxious to send them back to the less active churches they had come from—so they could spread the contagion of joy and excitement the Holy Spirit had brought to our own body.

It is not a new concept with me. Several pastors around the country have done likewise. Veteran church leader David du Plessis once counseled with a newly revived Christian who balked at the idea of returning to the lifeless church he had attended for twenty-two years. "You spent twenty-two years contributing nothing—even hurting your church," du Plessis admonished. "Now that you're able, why don't you go back and do something to *help* your church?"

The tabernacle lost a number of families—which in a way was our purpose—but God amazed me every week as He honored His Word in a literal way. As I sought my neighboring pastor's growth— spiritually and numerically—God continued to build our congregation spiritually and numerically as well. Our greatest success—spiritually, numerically, and financially—happened after we began actively obeying that odd little principle in 1 Corinthians 10:24.

I see two great tragedies in the church today. One is the "people quest": the overt, aggressive grasp for people, for the purpose of producing record numbers on Sunday school rolls, without any thought for the other man's sheepfold. I found in my own ministry that a church can grow on a foundation of impure motives; but a church can never truly explode spiritually without a biblical attitude toward the growth of the other Christian churches in the community.

The other great tragedy of the church, oddly enough, is the flip side of this "people quest"; it is our failure to realize that the church *is* people.

Before I built a wall I'd ask to know
What I was walling in or walling out.

(Robert Frost, "Mending Wall")

8

The People-Church

I sat with J. Robert Ashcroft, one of the veterans of the Pentecostal movement, in a hotel in Syracuse, New York. We were talking about building new churches, and he made a statement that still echoes in my mind: "Tommy, if I were to build a city church today, it would be a church without walls."

What Ashcroft had come to believe, after a lifetime of church ministry, is what every pastor and every layman needs to understand and believe and practice today: the church is not a building—it is people.

Jesus never told us to build buildings, or erect denominational signs, or look on the map to find population areas in excess of ten thousand and then build our churches there. He never authorized the building of a monument to a man or to a denominational machine.

Instead Jesus found men and sent forth men for the total purpose of winning men. This was nearly impossible for me to grasp as I struggled for prominence in Buffalo. Even as I reached out for the huge numbers of people, I did not understand that the church is people, not a building. Over and over again I saw to it that my congregation was committed to our building.

The early church, on the other hand, worshiped in existing buildings and houses. Pastors today are terrified of this concept. I know, because I was one of them. Home Bible studies have been held suspect by many pastors for years, because pastors are afraid the people will become committed to the home group and then won't come back to the church building to pay for the mortgage. Pastors feel pressured to protect their huge investments in mortar and stone, when God's method never included such an investment in the first place.

God never intended for people to become committed to the mortar and stone of the building, or to the denominational sign on the lawn out front. This is not the church. The church is people. If the building were to burn tomorrow, or if the denomination were to collapse, the church would go on. If there were never another corporate worship service, there would still be a church—for the church is *people*; not masonry, not paperwork.

In many cases the building is the very *raison d'être*. Pastors feel that if they are building an edifice, the congregation will develop a sense of responsibility to the church. What this attitude really says is that the pastor does not trust his congregation to commit themselves to his leadership and to Christ as the head of the church. Or perhaps he does not trust himself to be capable of garnering that trust—especially if he is trying to establish *his* ministry in the community instead of the Holy Spirit's. This pastor is rerouting the spiritual attention of his own flock—and because of his attitude, his church is missing the scriptural mark.

Sadly, in many ministries, the building has become the end as well as the beginning. Perhaps it is a tired cliché that the walls of the church seem to keep people out instead of bring them in. Still, it is often true.

Look at your church budget. If a church spends more than twenty percent of its income on buildings, it may be missing the purpose of God. The cost of those walls is supplanting the cost of reaching people—the walls are keeping people out!

Our money must be invested in people, in ministry to people, in outreach to people—for people are the church.

During the past few years, less than five percent of the tabernacle's income has been devoted to mortgage payments. Some might say we have been lax in paying off the mortgage. But there are so many things we have needed to do for God—so many ways to reach people's souls with that money every month—that the building has become the least important part of our ministry. We have not dumped dollars into publicity and promotion, but into new areas of ministry—a Bible school, an addict rehabilitation center, a new television ministry, a foreign missions program, and other outreaches—and only as the Spirit has specifically led us.

Of course the building is important; it is the house of God. But we refuse to let it become an end in itself. When we did feel God leading us to build a new sanctuary, it was after God had built the congregation, after we had utilized every bit of space we had, after the overcrowding had forced us to build or stop winning new souls.

From my standpoint as a member of the clergy I can firmly state that church buildings, like automobiles and houses, tend to become status symbols for preachers. I have heard preachers say, "I have the largest church building in my city, or my state, or my denomination." It is usually obvious by the tone of voice that the building has become a status symbol to the pastor. Many times the pastor has mortgaged the congregation beyond the point of reason, simply to build a monument to his own ministry on this earth.

I was guilty of this very sin. I took great pride in my building. I liked to preach in the largest church, the most beautiful sanctuary, and so on and so forth, parading my status symbol before the world.

But this is not our calling. We are not called to make a mark for ourselves. Jesus himself had a wonderful ministry on this earth, yet He never built a building, never left a material mark to prove He had contributed something. He left *people*.

We pastors are not building mortar and brick, we are building lives. When we put our efforts, our budgets, our ministries into people instead of building programs—even if that means worshiping in hotel ballrooms, school buildings, houses, rented halls—perhaps we will rediscover God's destiny for the church.

The church of the future must involve this concept. How does a pastor tackle the inner city? In New York City, people are afraid to go out of their apartment houses at night for fear of muggers and rapists. Yet in their apartments, they are the church.

Ron Haus, pastor of the Church on the Hill in Vallejo, California, goes a step further. The church is not only people, he declares; the church is the family.

"The family doesn't experience church whenever

they travel X-number of miles to a particular campus to meet with other families," he says."The family itself is a formation of the corporate body of Christ."

In fact, Haus says, he finds that several gifts of the Spirit are more practically applied within the home than in the church. The Holy Spirit can more specifically minister to the needs of the body when He is only speaking to three or four individuals at once. How specific can a prophetic message be—and still be edifying to all—in a corporate meeting of five hundred people? Family worship, rather, is the ideal place for the operation of the Spirit's gifts—because the family is the church.

So how would Paul the apostle build a church in New York City? Exactly as he did in Corinth and every other city. He never began with a building program. Instead, he began with people. He got people saved and committed to his leadership and to the leadership of the elders he appointed within the body. Paul never preached commitment to buildings. He preached commitment to Christ, through commitment to the leadership of the church.

And those church leaders did not build buildings but rather went into homes—to build the church in the hearts and homes of men. Paul saw to it that people became committed to the men who were appointed by God to lead the body. If Paul were still in business today, he would concentrate on people. He would build commitments, appoint elders, and then send them forth into their own neighborhoods to begin a thousand small prayer cells throughout the city—in factories, banks, office buildings, dining rooms, at all levels of society, in the ghetto, in suburbia—everywhere.

People were the church in the book of Acts.

People should be the church in the twentieth century. But we are so programmed to the building syndrome—and to the corporate meeting syndrome, which we wrongly see as a cure-all for weaknesses in the body—that we do not even come close to the church Paul established.

The church Paul established was in homes. It was so much a part of the home—and so little a part of the building—that some churches returning to biblical government today are doing away with one or more of the traditional corporate services that churches have relied on for so long. At this writing, for instance, Ron Haus and his church staff are praying about phasing out their Sunday night services at the Church on the Hill—to give more attention to the home cell meetings that are ministering so beautifully to the entire body.

"I'm not a predictor," Haus says, "but I predict that this is coming on the scene: the neighborhood invasion of the church." The old stereotype of the church, he says, "will phase out into something greater across America."

After all, Haus adds, the gathering on the church property by its very nature involves the tiniest time bracket of any function of the church. It follows, then, that the church building is the least important in terms of spiritual growth.

The tragedy of the building syndrome—though widespread—is by no means final. We can get the church back on course if we will get back to its scriptural basis—*people*. We must design our budgets around people, we must plan our programs around people, and we must focus our commitments on Christ—forgetting the age-old concept that the church is a building. *It is people*.

No person could have convinced me that *starting* a church explosion required *stopping* so much of what I was doing. But, just like the lilies of the field, I stopped toiling and spinning—and God began clothing our church with beautiful raiments. God had assured me that He would build His church, and I finally came to the place where I let Him do that. I simply turned the church and its program—the people and the building alike—over to God and let Him run it.

Today, to the natural eye, there is no program in

our church. There are no goals for attendance, no cardboard thermometers to measure our giving. God is accomplishing His purpose through His program—without the pastor jacking it up and tinkering with the works.

The people are delighted to be going with the flow. There is no tension in the worship service now. Where once we had to gear up for it with a little organ music, now we are already in it as we enter the sanctuary.

The Holy Spirit is flowing through us freely—individually and collectively—all the time. He doesn't wait for scheduled "revivals" or particularly emotional altar calls. He flows continually, because the church is His. We are obeying the toughest, yet the simplest, principle of church growth: Be in the middle of the flow.

Today, instead of pursuing cardboard goals, we are pursuing something else: the vision.

God began showing me that the vision I had been clutching desperately for seven years was only being put to half-use all that time—that once I surrendered my Isaac to Him, the vision could become a positive, aggressive instrument of faith.

When God gives a man a vision, the man must enter into that vision every day. If he will see his ministry *as God showed it to him*—if he will step into that visionary dimension day after day in his prayer closet, if he will live in that vision—God will bring it to pass.

There were times in my ministry when I could not have gone on any further—except for the vision. There were times when the church not only failed to grow but actually began to shrink. For a time the pews grew emptier and emptier Sunday by Sunday. I actually talked friends out of visiting my church because I was embarrassed by what was happening.

Yet it was these traumatic times that brought me to God's knee, to the learning place. It was here I realized that if the church ever did grow, it would be through God's grace and not my own ability.

So I came to live in that vision. I held onto it, like a drowning man clutching a scrap of wood in the middle of the ocean. It was all I had.

But since then, I have entered into a new dimension of living in the vision. I not only hold onto that vision, but now I pray in the vision. I visualize my church not as it is, but as God sees it. When God leads me to add a new program to the weekly schedule of services, I don't see the empty seats. Instead, I see that service as God showed it to me in the vision. Juggling the schedule to find the best time does not alter the vision. Even temporary cancellation does not make me give up on the vision. I pray for the program not as it is but as I see it in the eyes of God.

And without fail, God brings that vision to pass. The pews begin to fill, the program flourishes, the Spirit moves, and God's vision is fulfilled.

And how real it becomes! I minister to the church as God sees it—through the eye of faith, the eye of the future. I pray for the people who will fill the *next* sanctuary we are forced to build, and the people I will reach through the television ministry a *year* from now, and the students who will become part of our *expanded* Bible school program.

This is not the faddish "positive thinking" technique. It is the way Jesus prayed: "Neither pray I for these alone, but for them also which shall believe on me through their word; That they all may be one" (John 17:20, 21). Jesus was praying for us before we were even born. When I step into Christ's prayer dimension, I pray for people I have never seen, people who today would have no place to sit in our auditorium, people who have never heard of our Bible school, people who are not yet within the range of our television ministry.

There is indeed a goal in our church. The Holy Spirit has laid the goal for our church upon the hearts of the leadership. But it is a selfless goal: it does not depend on Tommy Reid or any other person. It is God's vision for His church.

The goal may not be realized in my lifetime. The goal may not be realized by Full Gospel Tabernacle at all. God may choose to let His Spirit flow to another sanctuary, another people, to reach the city of Buffalo.

But we will still go with the flow, even if that means going elsewhere.

I have a hard time praying what has become my major prayer in life: "Lord, help me to be willing if you ever want me to step down from the pulpit and into the prayer closet."

God's vision will be fulfilled, undeniably, for the Spirit will flow around a man if the Spirit cannot flow through him. The history of the Christian church clearly shows how men have wrongly stayed put when the Spirit has already moved on. There are dozens of accounts of church leaders whose ministries were wrested from them, because their ministries began to revolve around them. They were no longer going with the flow.

So, as I saw God beginning to work in the tabernacle, I began to pray every day: "Where will your Spirit flow today? How will your vision be fulfilled today?"

Where we once had been spinning our wheels as a church, now we had some forward motion. But now God wanted to push us beyond that, into a new time warp, where our entire concept of the church would be aligned with His original design—His vision of the church.

In the days that lay ahead, He would strip from my mind some of the oldest and most widely accepted notions about the church. He would replace them with jarring truths that would shake the foundations of the entire Buffalo ministry.

It is time for a new generation of leadership,
to cope with new problems
and new opportunities.
For there is a new world to be won.

(John Fitzgerald Kennedy, 1960)

9

The Threat of Eldership

God never intended churches to be small.

The early church was not small. It began with 120 and added 3,000 at a single sitting. Within days they had added another 5,000. Some scholars believe these figures represent men alone, not counting women and children. Which means they had 8,120 *at least* in the first few days of the New Testament church that we so proudly claim to be an extension of.

Hundreds of pastors today have programmed their people to believe in "family-sized" churches—anything over 500 is branded as "too impersonal." But that attitude is simply a rationalization technique for the spiritual underachiever. If the Holy Spirit is free to work, the church will explode. If God is in charge of the operation of the church, the church will explode just as the early church did. As for the problem of getting "too impersonal," God has a better solution for that.

God's vision is for His large churches to have a plurality of leadership—He never designed the single-pastor plan that we pastors hold so dear today. The Bible speaks of only one church in any given city. There was no First Church of Corinth, no East Side Church of Corinth, no Corinth Reformed Church of Christ. Paul ministered to *the church at Corinth*—all the believers in the city.

Of course Paul could hardly minister to so many thousands of people at once—no more than a single pastor can hope to minister single-handedly to an exploding church today. So Paul operated on God's governmental blueprint—a plurality of leadership: *government by elders.*

I was shocked to discover that the biblical pattern of church government—God's vision for the church—is being followed almost nowhere in the world today.

I knew from basic Bible school that there are four kinds of church government. The episcopal form calls for a bishop to control the churches in an area—as in the Roman Catholic and Methodist and Episcopal churches.

The congregational form calls for a democratic vote on leadership—as among the Baptists and

Congregationalists and the Assemblies of God.

The independent form calls for the pastor of the individual body to be its sole earthly authority—as in many interdenominational and nondenominational churches.

And the presbyterian form calls for the local church to be governed by a group of elders within the congregation—with one elder chosen by the rest to lead the church.

An objective look at church government is impossible for most believers, since our perception has usually been colored by a lifetime of experience with one form. So God must step in to blast away those years of preconceptions—and show us through the Scriptures the plan that He ordained, the plan that His people have misplaced along the way.*

The first principle God laid down in Scripture was that Christ is the head of the church. This is the specific foundation of all church government. This is the source of all the church's power. The church is not built on advertising or on visitation or on evangelistic programs. The church has only one energizer—Jesus Christ. The church is people, but the head of the body, its source of power and growth, is Jesus Christ. He has all authority.

---

* Roy Harthern, pastor of the exploding Calvary Assembly of God in Winter Park, Florida, was especially used of God to reveal the Scriptures to me on this subject. My special thanks to Roy for his kind help in the area of church government—as well as his friendship and fellowship in Christ.

This was tough for me to swallow. The authority of the church, I realized, is not vested in the pastor, nor in the presbytery, nor in the bishop's office, nor even in the people themselves. The ultimate authority of the church is vested in Jesus Christ alone.

But God works through His people. Jesus delegates His authority. All through Ephesians, Paul talks about Jesus as the head of the church, leading the rest of the body. Jesus delegates His authority to the arms and legs of the body.

At first Jesus delegated His authority to twelve disciples, and later to seventy others, and still later to hundreds of others, according to the following list: apostles, prophets, evangelists, pastors, teachers (Eph. 4:11). All of these received the delegated authority of Jesus Christ to do their part in equipping the entire body for the work of God.

Jesus said to His delegated disciples, "He that receiveth you receiveth me, and he that receiveth me receiveth him that sent me" (Matt. 10:40). This was also startling news to me: to receive Christ's authority requires receiving the authority of those in leadership positions in the body. Our attitude toward all leaders within the church is our attitude toward Christ himself.

But finally, in the most surprising revelation of all, God has shown many Christian leaders that His plan for this era of world history is to return biblical government to His church—a government of elders.

The role of the elder is spotlighted throughout the New Testament. In the King James Version, five different words—"elder," "bishop," "overseer," "pastor," "presbyter"—refer to this single role. These are the ones Paul instructed Titus to ordain in Crete (Titus 1:5). The apostle went on to list prerequisites for the job:

"For a bishop must be blameless, as the steward of God; not selfwilled, not soon angry, not given to wine, no striker, not given to filthy lucre; But a lover of hospitality, a lover of good men, sober, just, holy, temperate; Holding fast the faithful word as he hath been taught" (Titus 1:7-9).

In some churches today, the term "elder" suggests an administrator. In others it means a deacon, or a representative of the people to the pastor. But the scriptural meaning of "elder" is one of several people in any city who have been raised up *by God* to fulfill two responsibilities: to teach, both individuals and groups; and to labor among the people in one of the leadership positions Paul listed: teacher, pastor, evangelist, prophet, or apostle.

As a pastor, I am obviously threatened by this plan. These elders—several in every city—do the things I have done alone throughout my years as a pastor! How could God intend to split up the leadership of the church and give it to so many different people?

But God never intended one man to pastor thousands of people. One man might lead the thousands in corporate worship at certain times each week. But God's plan was to raise up men out of *the body itself* who would fill the various leadership roles in the church.

Today these "natural leaders"—the believers who tend to rise to places of leadership in the church—are almost universally relegated to teaching Sunday school classes. This is a tragic waste of the divine ideal. We need God-led Sunday school teachers, but God's plan more effectively uses the ones He anoints. His plan is more fulfilling for the individual and the body as well.

(Elders are also not to be bookkeepers. The Scripture specifically calls for *deacons* to be appointed to handle money matters.* Today's church has conveniently meshed the role of deacon and elder into one, counter to scriptural principle. Tension between pastor and board sometimes comes from the church's spiritual leadership and financial leadership being handled by the same group of men.)

If they don't only teach Sunday school, what do

---

* The term "deacon" literally means "servant," and in the early church the deacons played this role literally. They waited on tables—money tables—as they oversaw the distribution of the money in the church.

these elders do? In modern terms, they *are* the pastors of the church.

In the context of Scripture, it seems that a great portion of the teaching in the early church—as well as much of the worship—went on in the small meetings of believers in various neighborhood homes. Each meeting was led by an elder.

Even some of the most prominent and successful pastors have been leery of home meetings—either for fear the people will not pay off the bills on the church building, or for fear "they'll get off and start doing their own thing." Pastors often see home meetings as the place for dissension to begin. But as the Holy Spirit leads, this plan is God's ideal—the one God laid out for us in Scripture.

The early church met corporately each week, but they met in believers' homes and places of business all through the week. This is where evangelism took place. This is where discipleship took place. This is where *koinonia* and communion and personal ministries took place. The people were the church—literally—seven days every week, twenty-four hours every day.

Today we are raising a rootless generation. As soon as a young person hears the call of God on his life, we have conditioned him to feel he must launch out and find a ministry separate from the local body that nurtured him in the faith.

Under God's plan, the local body already has dozens of places to be filled by individual ministries.

Witness the common church directory. Inside the front cover is a big, beautiful portrait of the young man from the church who has accepted the challenge of "full-time ministry." He is in training to be a preacher. Buried in some obscure section of the booklet is the postage-stamp snapshot of the young man who teaches a Sunday school class, leads a home prayer meeting, organizes the youth rallies, supervises the outreach to the nursing home, drives the church bus, and ministers to the body of Christ in half a dozen other ways. This is the one that people shake their heads about: "Isn't it sad? He never even left home."

In the early church, young people were raised under eldership, trained for service in eldership, and eventually became elders themselves, leading home groups like the ones they had grown up in. Today we send our young people out—send them out to be trained by people who never saw them before, then require them to be licensed for the ministry by people who never saw them before, then expect them to minister to churches full of people who never saw them before. Several denominations promote this concept heavily, but it is directly contrary to God's vision of His church.

God designed the church and the family on the

same pattern. The children of a family are trained by the leaders within the family. The young people in our churches should be trained in a similar way. The children of a family are given responsibilities in growing measure by those who have trained them and have observed their lives close at hand.

We live in unevangelized cities today because we have sent all our evangelists away. In our church families, we have consistently violated the scriptural principle of family-type training.

Some pastors have tried to legislate biblical church government, concocting a system of legal checks and balances and procedures for nominating and electing elders. But the Bible says, "A man's gift maketh room for him" (Prov. 18:16), and on that basis I have literally let the Holy Spirit appoint the home prayer group leaders in the tabernacle.

Over and over, prayer groups have sprung up in believers' homes because believers felt the need to worship and learn and share together as the body of Christ.

Over and over I have had people in the church come to me with the news that one—or as many as four—prayer groups were already operating in their homes during the week.

It does not work any other way in our church. Several times I have tried to set up a home meeting—in a neighborhood without one, or in the home of a likely leader. Every one of these legislated home meetings—even one in my own home—has died an untimely death.

Eventually we began organizing to an extent. Although the home prayer cells are not governed by any written bylaws, and are not even officially a part of our church government, my associate pastors and I quiz each new home leader about his faith and then approve him or her to teach with the authority of our church. The home leaders are required to teach from a very basic Bible curriculum, but each group takes its own shape, develops its own complexion, establishes its own format.

Each also fills its own needs. A group including a majority of Catholics, or those with Catholic backgrounds, will focus on concepts of Scripture most helpful to these believers. Likewise, in groups made up of new converts, or local preachers, or other specific categories, we stress concepts related to them.

The only other requirement of home leaders is that they keep themselves in submission to the spiritual leadership of the church. If there are any problems in a ministry, my associate pastors and I investigate the situation and discipline appropriately. But even for these "rules," the entire body is a very informal, loosely organized structure.

The home group leaders and I meet each Wednesday for supper in the church basement—not to check in, but just to worship and share as fellow-believers. These leaders are ministering to others during the week, so this get-together allows them to relax and be ministered to.

One of our prayer group leaders calls the group "the perfect blend of beef stew." They don't look too great, but they complement one another beautifully. There are peas and potatoes and chunks of beef—all kinds of people, from all levels of society, representing all different theological tints.

Oddly, only a handful of prayer group leaders are people most pastors would have chosen as spiritual elders. The natural self tends to look for the successful businessman, the doctor or the lawyer, the career wife, perhaps the Cadillac drivers, or people from the higher-rent suburbs.

Instead, God has raised up leaders of His own make and model. As they chow down together from paper plates in the church basement, dressed in their sweatshirts and tennis shoes and baseball caps, they don't look particularly worthy to shepherd a flock. On Sundays they are as dressed as the rest of the church world. They are simply human beings. They are second-shift at the steel mill. They are an unshaven Jesus person. They are a construction worker, an Italian housewife, an occasional chef or printer. And yes, there are businessmen who drive Cadillacs. One man is also on the board of directors at the Catholic church in town. These are the spiritual leaders of our church!

Each one's gift has made room for itself. Each home leader is pastoring a cell within the body of Christ—and relationships between believers are growing, and this is strengthening the church.

The flip side of the eldership plan is the concept of the "single-church city." God intended every city to have a single great church—not under a single pastor, but under a *multiplicity of elders.*

When my neighboring pastors and I cooperate as if we pastor the same church—as we link arms and support each other's growth—we are coming closer to God's ideal. Each of us is still the head elder of his own church, but we are all co-elders of the body of Christ in the city of Buffalo. If we lived in the days of Paul, Titus might have ordained us to our responsibilities. We are only elders of equal stature in God's governmental blueprint.

It is not easy for an entrenched pastor to open his heart to God's way in this area. It is disconcerting and threatening, unless that pastor has surrendered his Isaac, unless he is going with the flow. Then it is a joyful experience, for the Holy Spirit is flowing all over the world in the same direction—toward the perfection of God's church.

In fact, I have talked for hours with many of the greatest church leaders of America, and God has spoken to every one of them, without exception, in the same way He has spoken to me. God's plan of eldership and home ministry has appeared in dozens of churches across the country and around the world. This has almost always occurred spontaneously, as the Holy Spirit has led church leaders back to the biblical plan.

Most of the churches in America that are already operating on the principles of biblical government have not, in fact, come to this place by any conscious drive on the part of outspoken church leaders, or even by word of mouth. Over and over I have met pastors who began establishing biblical government in their churches without the knowledge that anybody else in the world was doing the same.

Quentin Edwards, for example, was a successful evangelist, having preached to sixty thousand at a single time in India and hundreds of thousands in forty-three other nations of the earth. God led him to settle in Winter Haven, Florida, and take up the pastorate of the anemic First Assembly of God. The church was nearly fifty years old and its attendance averaged 160 people on Sunday mornings.

Edwards worked hard; he preached his famous fiery sermons, and the crowds flocked in. Before many months had passed, he had to move his services to the municipal auditorium. For two solid years he packed the place. Crowds of 2,500 were common. And in every service, regardless of the sermon topic, sinners always came to Christ.

"And then God dealt with me," Edwards says, "very emphatically." He began his sermon one morning by telling the story of a baby who was eaten alive by a hungry dog in a New York City apartment house. The mother had carelessly left the child and the dog in the apartment while she went out for a while.

Suddenly, in the midst of the story, the Holy Spirit fell on the preacher and showed him that he was carelessly letting the helpless believers fend for themselves too. He had been evangelizing week after week—winning souls—*without meeting the human needs* represented by the people who filled the altars.

"We are dumping babies on the doorstep," Edwards told his congregation as he began hammering on the subject in that very service. "We are nothing more than a huge day-care center for souls."

The grieved preacher began sharing with his church the need to feed souls and care for new converts—beyond simply raking them into the kingdom. "How are we shepherding them?" he cried.

It was the beginning of an explosion in that church. God showed Edwards that he could never care for those hundreds of babes in Christ by himself—but God would allow the pastor to reproduce himself, by way of biblical government, and minister to his flock through dozens of co-elders.

Instantly Edwards called a halt to altar calls. He began feeding the people in service after service, leaving evangelizing to the individual Christians. For twenty-one consecutive Sundays he taught nothing but concepts of discipleship—a series of sermons that today comprise a classic cassette textbook which has been instrumental in establishing hundreds of other biblically governed ministries as other men of God have tuned in to the concepts.

Today, First Assembly is called the Cypress Cathedral, a thriving church overseen spiritually by Pastor Edwards and an assortment of elders. The business of the church is conducted by deacons. And twenty home leaders are shepherding the people in their own neighborhoods every week.

The day-care services have disappeared. Today Quentin Edwards, the well-known preacher, prefers to be called simply a teacher. Biblical government in his church is fostering a beautiful, solid pattern of growth in both the pastor and the people.

It is clear that this is the age in which God will reestablish biblical government within His church. It is an urgent assignment He gives us. People are hurting, and God's plan for the church raises up people in the local congregation to help the hurting, to put their arms around the ones who need support, to pray with them and hold them up—not as pastors, acting out of some official responsibility, but as covenant brothers and sisters, acting out of Christ-like love.

God said in the last days He would pour out His Spirit upon all flesh (Joel 2:28). That is happening. Now we must deal with the avalanche. The typical, modern Superchurch, a monstrous architectural facility equipped for ministry to thousands, is only half the answer.

God's program of eldership—the ministry of elders throughout the body of Christ—is the answer. We don't have time to build the churches it will take to accommodate the new converts drawn in by this mighty outpouring of God's Spirit. We don't have the time or the money—or the need. God has provided the plan. And that plan is people—elders.

At this writing, the Full Gospel Church in Seoul, South Korea, has over seventy thousand adult members and is growing by two thousand adult members every month. Pastor Cho Younggi's vision is to have the largest church in the history of the Christian world within three years. His goal is one hundred thousand adult members.

How does it happen? It happens when the pastor opens his heart to the moving of the Holy Spirit and allows God to raise up nearly five thousand elders within the body. Those elders are pastoring home cell units and leading prayer groups all over the Seoul area.

One elder alone began five years ago in a suburban of only a few thousand people. He led about a dozen people to Christ, they formed a prayer cell and joined the church, and eventually God raised up an elder from the group. So the original elder went down the street and began the process again. He didn't start a new church—he started another neighborhood meeting. For corporate worship, they all participated with the believers *of the city* in Pastor Cho's services in Seoul.

The man kept moving on, from block to block, every time God raised up an elder in a neighborhood group. Today there are more than forty prayer cells in that suburb, with one elder each, representing a total of 640 members in the corporate church of Seoul!

The story is repeated again and again, all across America and the world, as pastors fall back on biblical church government: Karl Strader in Lakeland, Florida; J. Don George in Irving, Texas;

Bob Schmidgall in Naperville, Illinois; Gerald Fry in San Jose; Quentin Edwards; Ron Haus; Roy Harthern; and dozens of others. All these have discovered the secret of success by returning to the plan that God gave us—His vision—for the church.

But a church, like a business, can only rise to the level of its leadership. And as God broke me down—as He crushed my impure motives and my stiff-necked traditionalism—He opened my heart to one more mammoth idea. Before He was through with me, God had reached down and touched me in my most tender place—my wallet.

The holy passion of Friendship is of so sweet and steady and loyal and enduring a nature that it will last through a whole lifetime; if not asked to lend money.

(Mark Twain, *Pudd'nhead Wilson*)

10

The Common Purse

Communism frightens or infuriates, depending on the mind-set of the individual American. The socialist concept of a "state pot"—a pot that every individual contributes to and thrives on—runs counter to the principles of free enterprise, democracy, and capitalism.

That's why it drives American Christians to righteous distraction when a Bible scholar insists that the early church was socialistic. Nevertheless, many scholars do.

The early church did not, in fact, practice capitalism as we cling to it today. They were not dedicated to the every-man-for-himself concept. Instead, they lived for each other. Each lived his life for the benefit of the entire body of believers. *They were in covenant.*

The Bible says they broke bread together every

day. This was a symbol of the covenant, for bread is the "staff of life." The believers in the New Testament were engaged in a covenant relationship—exchanging their wealth, their energies, and their very lives.

The believers in the early church had all things in common—and yet today we overlook this portion of the divine truth. It is hard for the contemporary American Christian to swallow the fact that the early church was not democratic and not capitalistic. Both of these concepts are so much a part of the modern church, and modern America, that we forget to separate them from the truth of God's Word.

Still, on the basis of the early church pattern, we must enter into the covenant relationship not only with God but with our fellow-believers as well. Regardless of our trust in democracy, free enterprise, and the American way, we must share our money, our energies, and our very lives with the other believers in our church.

This is a devastating concept for the one who holds grudges, for the racial bigot, for the tightfisted. But the covenant concept is perhaps most difficult of all for the ones who must initiate it in every body of believers—the pastors.

Because a congregation can grow no further than its leadership, it is vital for pastors to become covenant-brothers in Christ with their associate pastors—as examples to their people, if not for the good it will do their own ministries.

In most large churches, the highly paid pastor has poorly paid associates. In one church in the north central United States, the pastor lived in a mansion, drove two Cadillacs, lived literally like a king. For a time he had an assistant pastor who, along with his wife, worked about fifteen hours a day at the church.

The husband played the organ and did the printing, the wife kept the church books, directed the church's entire music ministry, and typed the pastor's correspondence. Between them they answered the phones. They could be found working in the church office till midnight nearly every night, with their child in the hands of a babysitter.

And together they hardly made the salary of an ordinary factory worker.

When they finally left the church from sheer exhaustion, they had nothing of this world's goods. The pastor, meanwhile, was growing increasingly rich and influential.

Hundreds of churches duplicate this scenario to some extent. But as God dragged me through the Scriptures and showed me in so many ways how He intended to pattern my church after His church, I realized that pastors must be in perfect biblical covenant with their co-elders.

For most pastors, it is the first aspect of the

covenant that is hardest to accept: the exchange of garments, or wealth. Many preachers spend years pioneering tiny works, and when they finally receive a reasonable salary they are hesitant to part with it. But the covenant requires it. *Who owns Isaac?*

After I had been pastoring the tabernacle for some time, the people voted to replace my salary with a percentage of the church's income. As the church later began to explode, I realized this arrangement was going to be favorable for me, to say the least. I had no other financial security. I had felt led of God to give the church my rights to my aunt's property. Still, I was comfortable, and as my income grew beyond my need, I turned more and more of my pay back in to the church.

But as God began to deal with me about the covenant relationship, I suddenly realized that my co-elders and I were also in that relationship. What was mine actually belonged to them. That percentage was not mine alone—it was ours together.

If I wanted covenant relationships to develop in the body of the church, *they would have to begin at the pastoral level.*

And the place to begin was in that most sensitive area—the exchange of garments. That fund must then belong to my associates as well as to me.

No more chance of being financially independent.

No more chance of having an income equal to pastors of other churches the size of mine. My associates must share equally with me.

From that day since, my associate pastors and I have shared a common purse. We draw from it on the basis of need. In some years my associates have actually drawn more money from the common purse than I have. And that's the ideal. The common purse, like the covenant itself, is designed to meet needs.

The exchange of weapons, in its own way, also meets needs. As the head elder, I must also share my strength and energies with my co-elders. As David and Jonathan exchanged weapons, I must share with my co-elders every bit of my strength—and they must share theirs with me as well.

This exchange of strength is beautifully demonstrated as my brethren stick with me through all kinds of situations. Even in the trivial matters, or in the middle-of-the-night emergencies, my associates often take care of the problems without even calling me—because we share our strength. Rather than awaken me or call me from my family, they take care of my work. And I do the same for them.

Gone are my days as the kingpin pastor, when I took the "after all, you are my assistant" attitude. Today my associates are my co-elders. We are submitted to one another. They are not my servants. And, while I am their leader, I am not their king. Together we are all submitted to Christ as the head of the church.

Thirdly, the covenant requires an exchange of lives. This aspect of the relationship is actually a "death covenant." Just as Christ is in death covenant with His people, because He gave His life for us, I too as a pastor must be in death covenant with my associates. I must share my very life with my staff, because the covenant must be expressed first at the pastoral level before it can hope to be expressed throughout the body.

Perhaps we will never know the sum total of what the death covenant could mean in the context of our earthly relationships. Christ fulfilled the death covenant by dying on the cross. He took on the flesh of all mankind—He took on our fleshly sin—and let us live by way of His death.

By the same token, then, my co-elders and I can express the death covenant by taking on Christ's life—His holiness and righteousness—and letting Him live through us.

In order to express the death covenant fully, my co-elders and I must be the living embodiment of the presence of Christ. We must die to ourselves and allow Christ to live through us.

In my relationship with my co-elders, I must

express the nature of Christ, and, in essence, the nature of Tommy Reid must not be expressed. When I express selfishness, temper, greed, envy, or other manifestations of the flesh, I am living my own life in front of my co-elders. I am expressing my own life to them.

But because I am in death covenant with them, the life I express to them must be the Christ life—an expression of love, joy, peace, and longsuffering. For my covenant brothers, I must die to myself.

The result of God's death covenant with man was communication. Today you and I are able to go to the Father through Christ, because He exchanged His life for ours.

The result of my death covenant with my elders is also the establishment of communication—godly communication that keeps our hearts and minds pure and open to the leadership of Jesus Christ as the head of the church.

This expression of covenant on the pastoral level is vital to the future of the church. God expressed covenant with His people; pastors must likewise express covenant with their co-elders. By the same token, if our small cell groups were all covenant groups, we would no longer need benevolence offerings in our corporate worship services, we would no longer need food barrels standing in our church lobbies, because every family would be taken care of within its own covenant group. And if the small cell could not fulfill the need, then the church could assist.

Foodstuff fills only a fraction of the picture. People who need healing would be prayed for and supported not by the pastor on call that day, but by their covenant brothers and sisters. Others would find their covenant brethren sitting with them all night in the hospital. The shut-ins would find their needs taken care of from day to day, not by a visitation pastor but by their brothers and sisters in the covenant—the ones who live in their midst every day of the week.

But the Bible covenant community must start with the pastor and his relationship to his associates. Only when the pastor is willing to share his wealth, his energies, and his very life with his co-elders—in fact, only when the pastor is willing to *accept* his associates as co-elders in the first place—can God's scriptural pattern for the church be accomplished.

And that divine pattern is prerequisite to true church growth. I used to think church growth was a concept born of this century, and that super-growth was an even newer concept spawned by the seventies. But church growth in God's eyes is the inevitable outgrowth of a ministry that is flowing with God's Spirit.

Besides, God's eyes do not see what we see.

Church growth from His perspective is qualitative, not quantitative. Growth is not just mass—it is energy. *It is spirit.*

"Pure religion and undefiled before God ... is this, To visit the fatherless and widows in their affliction" (James 1:27). The church grows as pastors commit themselves to people, as believers commit themselves to one another, as the covenant relationship is exercised and grows strong in the members of Christ's body.

It can happen. This is God's hour for such a mighty move.

And when the day of Pentecost was fully come, they were all with one accord in one place.

(Acts 2:1)

The Church of Tomorrow

I can see the church of tomorrow emerging today.

It is not just another denomination, not just another reformation. It is not simply another swing of the spiritual pendulum, from an emphasis on faith to an emphasis on works, from Martin Luther to the holiness movement.

The church of tomorrow is not simply an outgrowth of the charismatic movement. It is more than a *Time* magazine cover declaring "The Year of the Evangelical."

The church of tomorrow will frighten some. It will destroy some old myths, many of which are as solid as the gospel in the hearts of good Christian men. The church of tomorrow will be shocking. But the church of tomorrow will be more like the Scriptures than any church of a past era. It will involve a return to normalcy that somehow has escaped

Christendom since the days of Paul and John.

The church of tomorrow will be catholic in concept—not a single, great organization operating under papal rule, but a worldwide body of believers who regard themselves as the universal church of Jesus Christ.

There are those who fear a world church as an open door for the Antichrist. But there are two world churches emerging—the false and the true. Satan always mimics God's handiwork—although he can never create the substitute before the original. The true world church, the church that is emerging today, is the one Satan will find worth imitating.

God created only one church in the New Testament. The world church is already a reality—it is already God's own. Only self-willed mankind has failed to realize this. Pastors going with the flow of the Holy Spirit are discovering this dramatic biblical premise of church existence as never before. In each city—and throughout the earth—there is only *one Christian Church*.

And we pastors are only multiple elders. For those who would move with God, the days of building empires are over. The days of sheep-stealing are gone. The shepherds are coming together, to be multiple elders over one flock. We will disciple together, we will love together, we will come to identify with the other elders in our own cities, and we will recognize the lordship of Jesus over us all.

The church of the future will bring the kingdom of God to its fullest beauty and power. We will be a truly universal church.

The church of the future will be people-oriented, not building-oriented. Once we recognize that we don't have to outdo Reverend Jones down the block and build a bigger monument than he's building, we will have lost our greatest incentive to start building programs. The church which today is slave to mortar and stone will become the servant of its people.

Those who sneer at the social gospel will be disgruntled, for the church of tomorrow will have a different budget, with more of its focus on social programs to feed the hungry and rehabilitate the downtrodden. Tomorrow's church will spend more money on soul-winning and less on attendance drives. We will return to the biblical concept including corporate worship *and* home worship, all as part of the one great program of God. The church of tomorrow will have the home as its altar, its classroom, its sanctuary.

The church of tomorrow will hardly have a choice. As the Holy Spirit is poured out in the last days, as pastors begin to surrender their Isaacs and go with the flow, our buildings will literally become too small to house the converts. Our inflated dollars will no longer build bigger sanctuaries for the sake of traditional corporate worship. God will drive us back to a people-oriented church.

And the church of tomorrow will be kingdom-oriented, not empire-oriented. Today, in city after city, each pastor and each religious organization is building an empire of its own. But in the coming years, as each pastor recognizes his co-eldership with other men of God in his city, he will no longer be interested in building his own empire. The denominations moving with the Holy Spirit will join hands. We will all get involved in building God's kingdom.

Some say these ideals are too high for the earthly church. Others find them too risky. Mankind, they say, inevitably spoils God's ideal.

But this church of which you and I are a part is not earthly. It is a heavenly organization. Its headship is at the right hand of the Father. It's corporate headquarters is in the celestial city. It's rule book is divinely authored. Its members are both terrestrial and celestial. It is headed not only for success, but for coronation as the bride of Christ.

We are seeing men's hearts melt together today in a unity never known since the first century. It is a unity that Jesus prayed for: "That they all may be one; as thou, Father, art in me, and I in thee, that they also may be one in us: that the world may believe that thou hast sent me. . . . That they may be made perfect in one" (John 17:21, 23).

His prayer is being answered today. The church of tomorrow is already happening.

One night God showed me the world from afar. The earth was dark, except for a few faint lights.

The lights were atop church steeples.

Each one lighted the little circle of ground around it.

One of those steeple lights was my own.

"That's my church!" I cried, pointing. "That's my church!"

Then God showed me the world again. The church steeples still lighted their little circles. But now there were other lights too.

I leaned down for a closer look.

These new lights were coming from homes.

"This," God said, " is *my* church."